AF321950

DATA STRATEGY
AND
AI VALUE CREATION

For Data Leaders by Data Leaders

DATA STRATEGY
AND
AI VALUE CREATION

For Data Leaders by Data Leaders

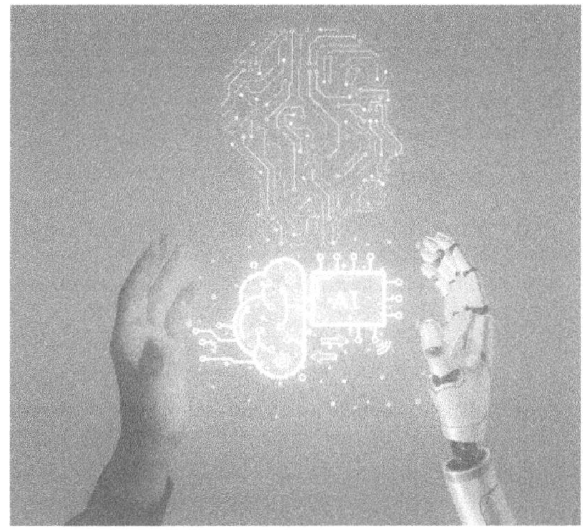

Edited by

Wai Fong Boh
Chee Hua (Neumann) Chew
Thara Ravindran

Nanyang Technological University, Singapore

NEW JERSEY · LONDON · SINGAPORE · BEIJING · SHANGHAI · TAIPEI · CHENNAI

Published by

World Scientific Publishing Co. Pte. Ltd.

5 Toh Tuck Link, Singapore 596224

USA office: 27 Warren Street, Suite 401-402, Hackensack, NJ 07601

UK office: 57 Shelton Street, Covent Garden, London WC2H 9HE

British Library Cataloguing-in-Publication Data
A catalogue record for this book is available from the British Library.

DATA STRATEGY AND AI VALUE CREATION
For Data Leaders by Data Leaders

ISBN 978-981-98-0084-1 (hardcover)
ISBN 978-981-98-0085-8 (ebook for institutions)
ISBN 978-981-98-0086-5 (ebook for individuals)

For any available supplementary material, please visit
https://www.worldscientific.com/worldscibooks/10.1142/14040#t=suppl

Desk Editor: Venkatesh Sandhya

Typeset by Stallion Press
Email: enquiries@stallionpress.com

Introduction

1. Context

We have been living with data and artificial intelligence (AI) for decades. AI needs data as fuel. We know and use data. We know about and have been subjected to AI predictions (e.g., bank loans, insurance claims, credit card transactions, and hospital services). However, two recent events changed the way most people viewed data and artificial intelligence — COVID-19 and generative AI.

COVID-19 highlighted the importance, power, and limitations of data. Data are important as the critical ingredient for understanding the actual situation. How contagious is the coronavirus? How deadly is COVID-19? What is the difference between COVID-19 and the seasonal flu? Expert opinion is one thing, but data provide the foundation. Experts need data to form their opinion and justify their recommendations. The public needs data to understand the actual situation and accept/reject assumptions, information, and actions to take.

The need for timely and accurate data is felt more acutely now than before. The lack of data perpetuates powerlessness and hearsay. Underestimated data build complacency; overestimated data spread exaggerated fear. Decisions by governments, hospitals, businesses, and citizens need timely, accurate, relevant data. The quality of data could mean the difference between life and death, prosperity and bankruptcy. However, the lack of data could be as destructive as wrong data. Thus, the power of data is felt in times of great stress and uncertainty.

In response, in addition to governments and international bodies, some universities, medical centers, and data repositories started collecting and publishing data on COVID-19. But data collected by one party might not be relevant to or sufficient for use by another. Often, the purpose and objectives of different parties may not be the same. The parties providing and using the data may not even know each other. Sooner or later, one may realize that data definitions are not the same, even if different parties use the same variable name. This can happen for data in different systems and even data that come from the same database. Furthermore, some units of measurement are inconsistent. If a data provider cannot provide all the data that one requires, perhaps we could combine our data with data from a third party? But this is easier said than done. Different datasets on the same entities cannot be merged due to a lack of common matching criteria. We cannot see the full picture with isolated pieces of datasets. Thus, we know that important information exists but it is locked and fragmented. There must be a way to see the full picture, but we do not know how, even if we can download related datasets from multiple sources. While we are empowered by data, we are also limited by data and the way they are recorded. Gaining access to data is one thing, but extracting insights from data is another.

The devil is in the details and in the implementation of data systems. But the problems with data that we face today seem to be the same as those faced by data leaders 100 years ago, albeit at a greater volume and velocity now. Hence, this book aims to rephrase the problems of our time and provide ideas and solutions that could help forge better management of data at present.

In contrast, our ability to extract insights from data has grown by leaps and bounds, especially with the arrival of the machine learning and AI era. In modern societies, we are subjected to the results of machine learning and AI models in our everyday life, even if we do not realize it. A model determines whether someone gets a bank loan or not. A model determines the insurance premiums someone has to pay after another model agrees that he/she is of acceptable risk. A model determines how long a patient can wait to see a doctor at the emergency room. Recently, a US judge decided on a sentence based on the results of a model. We are getting better at extracting insights from data by using machine learning and AI models invented in the last few decades. AI and machine learning have progressed by leaps and bounds, and now there is a new star in the AI space — generative AI.

Generative AI, and ChatGPT in particular, is very popular because it is proving the usefulness of AI and anyone can use it. Auto-generated text, sounds, and pictures are useful in many ways to many people, but the excitement is because anyone can use it for free, thereby offering endless potential. We are no longer just subjected to AI, but we could use AI ourselves to do work faster, better, and cheaper. Data leaders who have not been following the progress of machine learning and AI will have a lot to catch up on in order to understand the usefulness, potential, limitations, and dangers of non-generative AI and generative AI. Hence, this book is an attempt to explain in simple terms and in a business context the use and potential of non-generative and generative AI after which the limitations and dangers can be inferred.

2. Purpose and Intended Audience

The purpose of this book is as follows:

- To rephrase the ever-present problems of data in modern terms and context;
- To explain the management ideas and approaches that had proven useful in managing the problems of data;
- To explain in simple terms and in a business context the use and potential of non-generative and generative AI;
- To suggest how organizations could use non-generative and generative AI correctly.

For example, there are several similar data strategy books that have been written by external consultants from a single-person point of view (Bernard Marr, 2021). In contrast, our edited volume has been written by many internal data leaders working in various organizations, across different industries, with significant long-term responsibilities to stakeholders.

There are also several good books that explain how machine learning and AI models work. One such excellent book is by Gareth James *et al.* (2021). This book has been written by Stanford professors as a simplified treatment of their original textbook *Elements of Statistical Learning* and is meant for practitioners and executives. Alas, in this simplified work, the mathematical level is still much too high for most corporate executives, as it is too focused on techniques and not enough on the big picture. Our edited volume will fill this void by focusing on real business problems and opportunities and the big picture. Our book will indeed be suitable for all corporate executives and does not require a background in math, statistics, or programming.

With the rise in AI (both non-generative and generative), the synergy between data and AI is more apparent than ever before. Data contain non-obvious insights that can be effectively extracted via AI. The search for insights drives better management of existing data and acquisition of new data. This book helps explain the two themes and, toward the end, the synergistic features of data and AI.

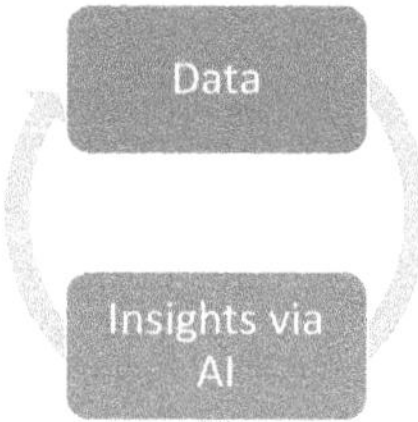

The intended audience for our book includes the following: all data leaders such as CEOs, CIOs, CDOs, heads of analytics, data scientists, and directors; business analysts and strategists responsible for identifying opportunities by leveraging data and AI; professionals defining use cases that deliver business value; risk and compliance officers who ensure that data strategies and AI initiatives comply with regulatory requirements and industry standards; those who may be concerned about the potential risks associated with data usage and AI use and need to develop strategies to mitigate the risks; and managers who identify opportunities related to the use of data and AI, who plan, execute, and implement data and AI initiatives.

Ensuring a robust data strategy and effective utilization of AI requires collaboration among professionals across various disciplines, and thus this book will benefit any professional who is interested in better governance, data strategies, and AI initiatives that can help their business.

3. Two Themes, One Objective

This book follows the two different but mutually reinforcing themes that are pervasive in industry leaders' practice: (1) data strategy and governance and (2) AI value creation. Data per se are just a collection of facts, opinions, and assumptions with *greater* potential and value if insights can be extracted correctly for specific purposes.

The keyword is "greater." All organizations are capable of analyzing their data and extracting information and insights. But how many organizations can reach the full potential of their data? What should we be doing to extract greater value and realize greater potential?

In terms of data strategy and governance, we focus on intentionally managing and using data effectively to achieve specific objectives. In terms of AI value creation, we focus on the use of artificial intelligence to generate business or social value. The common objective is to improve data-driven decision-making.

The organization of the book can be visualized using the following sunburst chart:

With regard to data, we focus on (a) data strategy and (b) data governance. Data strategy starts with the vision and goals for the use of data in organizations and delineates both the offensive and defensive use of data. Importantly, the support structure required to sustain a data strategy is proposed. In data governance, we turn to the operational aspects of data. How do we measure the quality of data? What do we measure? How do we assess the impact of data quality? How can we ensure both data privacy and effective use of data? What is considered acceptable use vs unacceptable use in a principled manner?

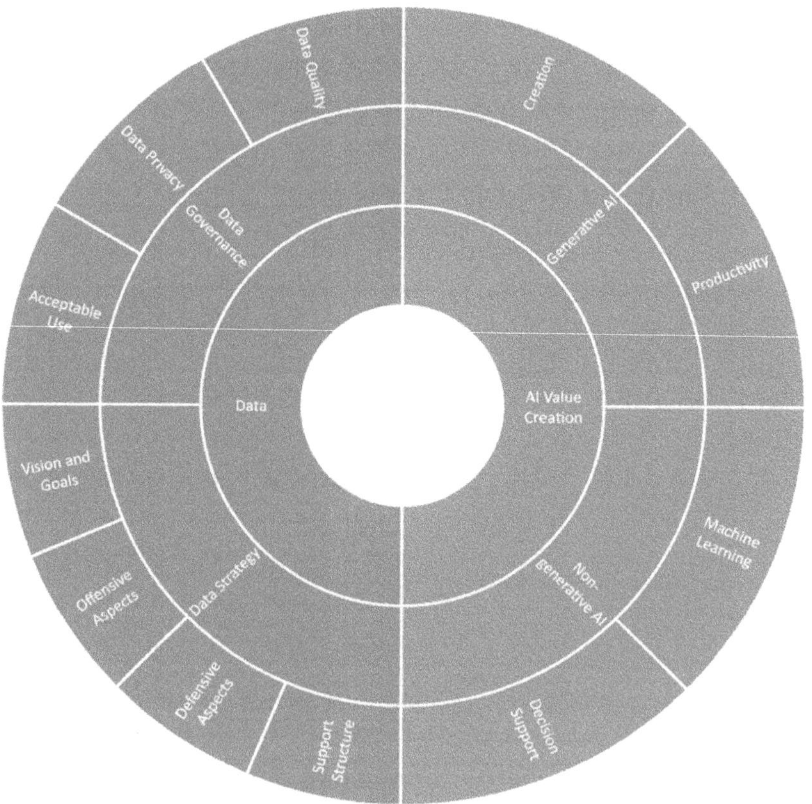

With regard to AI value creation, we explain the use, potential, and limitations of both non-generative AI (that has been in use for decades to support decision-making via machine learning) and generative AI (that creates new content and tremendously enhances productivity for some tasks). We have, however, skipped the mathematical and code details as they can be more effectively covered in specialized textbooks.

In the chapters that follow, the authors bring their expertise and decades of real-world experience to tell us what is important, what to watch out for, and how to succeed.

References

James, G., *et al.* (2021). *An Introduction to Statistical Learning: With Applications in R*, 2nd edn. Springer, USA

Marr, B. (2021). *Data Strategy: How to Profit from a World of Big Data, Analytics and Artificial Intelligence*, 2nd edn. Koganpage.

Contents

Chapter 1

Overview of the Chapters on Data Strategy and Governance

C. H. Neumann Chew

*Nanyang Business School, NTU Singapore,
91 Nanyang Avenue, Academic Building South (Gaia),
#06-18, Singapore 639956.
neumann.chew@ntu.edu.sg*

Keywords: Data, Data Strategy, AI, Data Governance, ChatGPT.

Data are a core asset that need to be intentionally managed for value in use and integrity. The COVID-19 pandemic highlighted the importance, power, and limitations of data. In particular, everyone realized and understood the following at a much deeper level:

- Data must be timely. The "battle" is lost if key decision-makers do not have data in time to make decisions.
- Data must be accurate. Wrong or grossly under/overestimated data lead to bad decisions. People can die and businesses can fold due to inaccurate data.
- The right data to the right person. The data needs of different persons vary. We need to ensure the right data at the right granularity can be accessed by the right person.

- Certain data must be shared. Without access to critical data held by selected parties, efforts cannot be coordinated and outcomes cannot be optimal. But how do we share data in an effective and controlled manner?
- The value of data lies in the use of data. Data per se are just raw information. We need to extract insights from data to reveal the key information that affects outcomes. What processes and support structures can be set up to facilitate a successful data–insights–outcomes loop?

The above-mentioned points can be addressed under two subareas of data — data strategy and data governance. The former deals with the strategic aspects of data [the why], while the latter deals with the operational aspects of data [the what and how].

1. What Is Data Strategy?

Data strategy is not well defined. A strategy does not become a data strategy just because it involves data.

ChatGPT 3.5 says "Data strategy is the comprehensive plan that organizations develop to manage, govern, and utilize their data assets effectively to achieve their business objectives. It involves making informed decisions about how to collect, store, process, analyze, and leverage data across the organization." This is too general. We need to be more specific and intentional about data strategy.

Over several decades, data strategy discussions evolved from just the platform used to collect, process, and analyze data (think databases, data warehouse, cloud computing, real-time processing, etc.) to a more fundamental reflection of the "strategy." Why does a specific organization need specific data and how do we facilitate and support the data strategy? The clarity of the "strategy" element is critical as it cascades down to everything we need to do, aspire to do, and should do about the data.

2. People and Process Issues Cause Analytics and AI to Fail

Over the years, we often hear reports on the increasing pace and magnitude of investment in data and AI. But the sobering results of a 2019 survey (Bean and Davenport, 2019) among C-suite executives of large corporations across industries revealed the following:

- 72% have yet to forge a data culture.
- 69% have not created a data-driven organization.
- 53% are not yet treating data as a business asset.
- 52% are not competing on data and analytics.
- Only 7.5% cited technology as the challenge.
- An overwhelming 93% cited people and process issues as the obstacle.

Thus, we need to focus on the people and process issues. Not the technology, code, or math. There are good ways to address these issues and it starts with data strategy.

3. Data Governance Has a Negative Connotation

Data strategy is an exciting topic for many. But the mood changes when we shift to data governance. Data strategy focuses on returns, while data governance focuses on risk. Thus, some Chief Data and Analytics Officers (CDAOs) avoid the term data governance when discussing specific data issues.

But returns and risk in an uncertain world are two sides of the same coin, i.e., risk cannot be avoided. But we can do better to link risk to returns instead of treating risk and returns as two isolated terms.

ChatGPT 3.5 says "Data Governance is a comprehensive framework and set of practices that ensure high data quality, data management, data security, and compliance within an organization. It involves defining and implementing policies, procedures, and standards to ensure that data is well-managed throughout its lifecycle." The keyword compliance seldom elicits excitement.

A good link between data governance and data strategy is via data quality. It shows how purposeful data governance leads to better data quality, resulting in better outcomes from the data strategy. Thus, data governance is necessary and good for everyone in the organization. This connection is made explicit in this book.

4. Scope

We begin this book by defining data strategy and showing examples of successful data strategies. Then, we discuss data quality, linking it to data strategy and data governance before discussing two aspects of data governance — data security and data privacy. Finally, we discuss the growing importance of data sharing, spearheaded by the EU government with key takeaways for non-EU data leaders.

The following authors were deliberately selected to authoritatively discuss these aspects of data strategy and data governance (Legner and Pentek, 2024; Rosich and Rüst, 2024; Kumar, 2024; Ray, 2024; Sowmya, 2024, Hartmann *et al.*, 2024).

Data Strategy begins with an organization's vision and goals for its data. Legner and Pentek (2024) define data strategy and explain the essential elements of a data strategy plan. This chapter highlights that both the defensive and offensive aspects of a data strategy plan should be addressed. Importantly, the resources and organizational structure necessary to support the data strategy must be planned for. In the end, nine recommendations are provided to "effectively develop and implement a data strategy."

The growing importance of data, their impact on business, and the critical success factors for managing data are explained by Rosich and Rüst (2024). The offensive and defensive aspects, together with the supporting structures across various successful data-driven organizations, are further illuminated. The capabilities that organizations should develop and the attributes they should nurture are explained with examples. This chapter provides real-world examples of successful data strategy.

The above-mentioned two chapters show the potential returns from data. In the next chapter, Kumar (2024) looks at the risk side of data. After defining data quality issues as "an intolerable defect in a dataset … that … reduces the reliability and trustworthiness of that data," we examine the potential causes and explain the best practices to manage data quality issues. However, data quality issues are not the only data issues of concern. In addition, with the rise of IoT, sensors, apps, online transactions, and AI, the acceptable use of data should be carefully planned. The wrong use of data, whether intentional or unintentional, creates additional risks for the organization.

The risks from data and the consequent laws and regulations are further explained by Ray (2024). Data are an asset to the company that owns/stores the data and for data attackers too. Contrary to popular belief, data security is not difficult if one can answer 6 simple data access questions. "Organizations who successfully implement data security practices … solve for security, not simply compliance." This chapter ends with a list of simple questions to evaluate the maturity of an organization's data security.

Next, Sowmya (2024) focuses on data privacy. Data privacy is associated with the concept of digital trust and, thus, is important for modern businesses and online transactions. Data privacy can be achieved even though different companies have to process the same customer data, e.g., patient hospital bill information and transactions across the hospital, bank, and insurer. Different companies can participate, check, and process a transaction chain without knowing the identity and other information non-essential to the transaction. This technology was already in use way before blockchain. Altogether, four different privacy-enhancing technologies are described at the right level of detail for non-privacy experts to understand. Perhaps one or more such technologies could be useful to your organization.

Lastly, the need to co-share and co-use data with other organizations takes on a much bigger scale [than the interested parties' patient bill example] in the EU with laws pushing for the use of "dataspaces." Hartmann *et al.* (2024) tell us about the latest initiatives in the EU and the development of company-level dataspaces that serve as "a trusted platform to exchange data." The benefits and issues are elucidated with specific examples. For non-EU data leaders, key takeaways are provided.

Together, we hope data leaders (anywhere) will find these chapters enlightening and useful for their organizations.

We have deliberately excluded math, software code examples, and technology implementations in order to focus on people, ideas, processes, and supporting structures. Thus, this book will not explain the mathematical details of models, programming, and technological details for which one can read other specialized books.

References

Bean, R. and Davenport, T. H. (2019). Companies are failing in their efforts to become data-driven. *Harvard Business Review*.

Hartmann, M., Baumann, F.W., and Lederer, E. (2025). Data Strategy and AI Value Creation: Dataspaces — Opportunities with ESG, Data Strategy and AI Value Creation, World Scientific.

Kumar, R. (2025). Challenges and best practices associated with data quality and acceptable use of data, Data Strategy and AI Value Creation, World Scientific.

Legner, C. and Pentek, T. (2025). Data strategy — Transforming into a data-driven enterprise, Data Strategy and AI Value Creation, World Scientific.

Ray, T. (2025). Personal data privacy, industry data regulations, and data security — Three sides of the same coin, Data Strategy and AI Value Creation, World Scientific.

Rosich, M. and Rüst, C. (2025). Unlocking the power of data: Key strategies for success, Data Strategy and AI Value Creation, World Scientific.

Sowmya, G. K. (2025). Privacy-first design — The significant role of privacy-enhancing Technologies, Data Strategy and AI Value Creation, World Scientific.

Chapter 2

Data Strategy — Transforming into a Data-Driven Enterprise

Christine Legner[*,‡] and Tobias Pentek[†,§]

*Faculty of Business and Economics (HEC), University of Lausanne, CH-1015 Lausanne, Switzerland
†CDQ AG, Lukasstr. 4, CH-9000 St. Gallen, Switzerland
‡christine.legner@unil.ch
§tobias.pentek@cdq.com

Abstract

Many companies recognize the strategic importance of data but realize that it takes time to transform their organization's approach to data. A data strategy — as a strong enterprise-wide framework for all data-related activities — is needed to guide this transformation. Still, it is often unclear what an effective data strategy is made of. In this chapter, we provide a definition of data strategy and outline its building blocks as well as how it links to other corporate strategies. Drawing from an analysis of data strategies of over 30 firms, we offer practical recommendations and a checklist to effectively develop and implement a data strategy.

Keywords: Data strategy, data monetization, data governance, data culture, data-driven enterprise.

> Companies that have not yet built a data strategy and a strong data management function need to catch up very fast or start planning for their market exit — (DalleMule and Davenport, 2018).

1. Motivation: Why Do Companies Need a Data Strategy?

Data's strategic role in shaping innovative business models and harnessing artificial intelligence is widely acknowledged. Consequently, most companies have increased their investments and launched data-focused initiatives to exploit analytics and foster innovation through data. Yet, only a few companies manage data with the same systematic and professional rigor as they do traditional corporate resources like financial, human, or physical assets. Even thought leaders, who fully recognize the role of data as a strategic asset, realize that transforming an organization's approach to data is a gradual and time-consuming process. A data strategy is seen as a cornerstone in driving this transformation. Still, it is often unclear what a data strategy should comprise and how it helps to unearth value from the "treasure troves" of data that exist in businesses today.

In this chapter, our goal is to guide companies and their management teams in the effective development and implementation of a data strategy. To achieve this, we address four key questions:

- What is a data strategy and what are its constituent elements?
- How does a data strategy integrate into the corporate strategy landscape and align with business, digital, and IT strategies?
- What experiences and good practices are out there that aid the development and implementation of data strategies?
- How can we justify developing a data strategy? And what arguments can be used to find allies and sponsors for the development of a data strategy within my company?

Our insights come from our research in the Competence Center Corporate Data Quality (CC CDQ), which brings together data experts from 20 multinational companies and researchers for the purpose of co-innovation and joint development of concepts, methods, and tools in the field of data management (Legner *et al.*, 2020). To elucidate the role and components of a data strategy, we start by reviewing concepts from the extensive body of strategy literature and applying them to the domain of data. Next, we provide a practical illustration of the development and implementation of a data strategy through a real-world example. We conclude with practical recommendations and a checklist that businesses can use when implementing their data strategy.

2. What Is a Data Strategy?

The term data strategy has not been defined well in the past. Although frequently referenced by practitioners, there is a scarcity of scholarly publications on the subject, and a precise and widely accepted definition is yet to be established. To offer a thorough understanding of a data strategy and its components, we build upon the extensive body of literature on corporate strategy and examine how this broader strategic framework can be specifically applied to the domain of data.

2.1. *The Concept of Strategy and How It Applies to Data*

The word "strategy" is derived from the Greek word "strategos" or the "art of army command." In a business context, a strategy specifies the medium- and long-term orientations with which a company achieves its goals and secures economic success. Developing a strategy involves establishing goals and defining in which direction the company should evolve. Crucially, a strategy must delineate the essential resources required to attain the defined set of goals and specify the organizational structure necessary to support and execute these goals effectively ("structure follows strategy") (Chandler, 1962).

In practical situations, there is a common risk of labeling any decision or fundamental direction as "strategy," which can lead to diluting its significance. Furthermore, many examples exist where strategies are poorly defined, consisting of superficial and vague statements, or goals are set without accompanying guidelines or measures. In his seminal book *Good Strategy/Bad Strategy*, Rumelt (2011) elucidates common misconceptions about corporate strategy and identifies three core elements of a "good" strategy:

- a diagnosis of the current situation and business challenges,
- a guiding policy to address these challenges,
- a set of coherent actions to implement.

These general understandings and guidelines for corporate strategies offer a valuable framework for a data strategy: Developing a data strategy should start from the diagnosis of the current situation and business challenges to define a vision, objectives, and guidelines to address these challenges. It also involves formulating a coherent set of actions to achieve these goals.

2.2. *Definition and Essential Elements of a Data Strategy*

In one of the few articles on the subject, DalleMule and Davenport (2018) emphasize the importance of a data strategy as well as two key themes that every company must address to succeed with data: *Defensive aspects* address the goal of being able to exercise control over data, ensuring aspects such as data security, data protection, and data quality. On the other hand, *offensive aspects* emphasize the various ways data can be used to generate business value. Hence, an effective data strategy must answer two central sets of questions:

(1) To address the offensive aspects, a data strategy needs to clearly articulate how a company plans to utilize data to generate

business value directly or indirectly. This is also referred to as *data monetization* and should not be confused with merely selling data (Wixom *et al.*, 2023). Instead, it underscores the measurable and tangible business value created through data. Typical forms of data monetization involve the derivation of insights using analytical methods, utilizing data to automate business processes and enhance operational performance, and the introduction of innovative digital products and services to generate new revenue streams.

(2) For the defensive aspects, a data strategy must explicitly define how a company intends to handle the collection, storage, processing, and management of data. This *data foundation* is essential to support data monetization efforts and generate business value. The data foundation encompasses critical topics like data quality, data governance, data architecture, and specific applications that make data available company-wide (e.g., a master data management hub or a data catalog). It also establishes guidelines to ensure the compliant and ethical use of data. The data foundation must be designed depending on which form of data monetization is chosen and which requirements result from this (e.g., regarding the scope, updating, or analysis of the data).

Building on these considerations, we can now define a data strategy as follows:

A data strategy is a *comprehensive plan* for how an organization should utilize and manage data to deliver business value directly or indirectly. It offers a *vision and objectives* and delineates *guidelines and a coherent set of actions* for realizing these objectives, encompassing both *data monetization* (offensive aspects) and *data foundation* (defensive aspects).

When developing the data strategy and answering these two questions, it is important to consider the maturity of the company. For instance, many companies encounter challenges in implementing

IoT scenarios because they cannot capture and process data feeds from smart devices due to a lack of a suitable data foundation. Moreover, AI use cases depend on the availability of high-quality datasets for training underlying models. As such, a data strategy must lay the groundwork for establishing fundamental data capabilities to ensure that the required datasets are collected and processed as a first step, so as to enable their subsequent utilization in the development of digital products and services.

2.3. *Data Strategy in the Context of Other Corporate Strategies*

It is important to note that the data strategy creates an enterprise-wide framework for data that can incorporate sub-strategies such as a data management strategy (emphasizing the data foundation and specifically data governance) or an analytics or AI strategy (emphasizing data monetization through analytical methods and specifically AI).

A data strategy, however, does not operate independently within a company. To achieve success, it must be seamlessly integrated into the corporate strategy landscape and closely aligned with other key strategies. This includes the company's corporate strategy, its digital strategy, IT strategy, as well as functional and divisional strategies (Fig. 1).

- *Data vs. corporate strategy*: Given that the corporate strategy defines the medium- and long-term orientations of the company, it also sets the framework for the data strategy. More precisely, the data strategy plays a contributory role in achieving the strategic corporate goals and should be derived from the overarching corporate strategy.
- *Data vs. digital strategy*: There is a subtle yet crucial distinction between data and digital strategy, and it is essential to regard them as complementary. A digital strategy can be embedded in the corporate strategy or can be addressed separately. It typically encompasses both internal digitalization, involving the

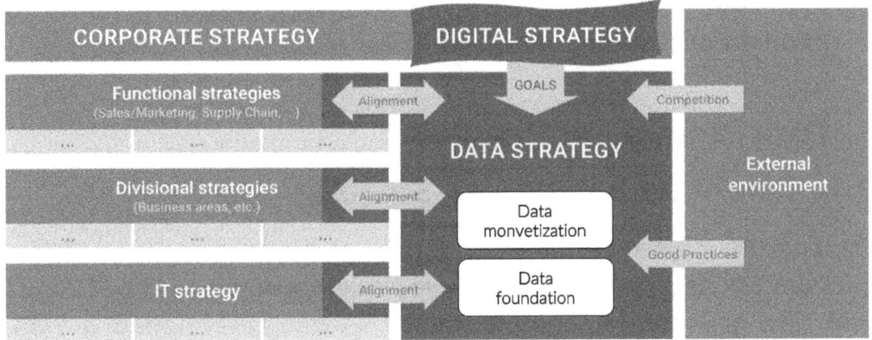

Fig. 1.   Data strategy in the context of corporate strategies.

organization and its employees, and external digitalization, focusing on strengthening digital channels and developing digital business models. A digital strategy thereby imposes specific requirements on data that must be considered in the development of the data strategy.

- *Data vs. functional and divisional strategies*: Additionally, functional and divisional strategies also place requirements on data, while, conversely, the goals and guidelines of a data strategy must be taken into account in functional and divisional strategies. Mature companies define cornerstones in their company-wide data strategy, which are then further detailed and substantiated in functional data strategies. For example, an HR data strategy focuses specifically on all employee data, while a data strategy for purchasing looks specifically at the data relevant to supplier relationships. Depending on the company, there may also be divisional data strategies for individual business areas.

- *Data vs. IT strategy*: The successful implementation of a data strategy hinges on its close interlinkage with the IT strategy. The latter defines the foundational elements of applications and IT infrastructure, which are crucial for supporting the data-related activities in the company. Overlaps in content and responsibilities, especially concerning areas like data architecture or the enterprise analytical platform, must be clarified and clearly resolved in the respective strategies.

3. Data Strategy in Practice

3.1. *Where do companies Stand?*

Despite the increasing interest in data and analytics, data strategies are not as commonplace as you may think. Bean (2021) finds that "few companies — only 30.0% — have developed a well-articulated data strategy." A survey of the Competence Center Corporate Data Quality (CC CDQ) reveals that two-thirds of the companies are developing a data strategy for the first time or have developed their first data strategy in the last few years (Legner and Pentek, 2021). Many of the most mature companies embarked on their data strategy journeys a decade or more ago, framing them initially within the context of master data or business intelligence strategies. These strategies have evolved in iterations since then. Mature companies also engage in regular strategy reviews to track the progress of their data-related activities, as well as the KPIs and the financial value created.

3.2. *Example: PMI's Dual Data Strategy*

The journey of Philip Morris International Inc. (PMI) to becoming a data-driven company serves as an exemplary illustration of a comprehensive data strategy, intricately linked to the broader business strategy and covering both offensive and defensive aspects (Fadler *et al.*, 2020). This journey, implemented over a three-year horizon, also throws light on the typical building blocks of a data strategy.

Data as a key enabler in PMI's business transformation. The starting point in developing a data strategy at PMI was a radical change in the company's strategy from traditional tobacco sales via wholesalers to a "smoke-free future." Since 2016, PMI has fundamentally transformed its business model with the goal of offering better alternatives to the consumer in the form of smoke-free products — such as the IQOS electronic tobacco heater. The move toward a

Table 1. Vision, mission, and goals of Enterprise Analytics & Data.

Vision	A data-driven PMI transition toward a smoke-free future: Every Decision. Every Day. Driven by Data.
Mission	Accelerate our customers' decisions through data-driven insights: Instill trust, knowledge, and full usage of our data.
Ambition	Generate 5 times more business value for PMI than EAD costs in 3 years.

B2C business model and the creation of a digital business function required PMI to better understand and respond to consumers' changing needs. Thus, data played a key role in PMI's strategic shift. As with many traditional companies, however, data proved to be both a challenge and an opportunity: On the one hand, data offered the opportunity to transform PMI's business by better understanding consumers, personalizing interactions with consumers, improving internal processes, products, and services, and strengthening fact-based decision-making. On the other hand, data remained a challenge because of data silos, data duplication, multiple sources of truth, and a lack of corporate-wide perspective on data. Top management recognized that data played a central role in the transformation of the core business and decided to establish a new organizational unit — Enterprise Analytics & Data (EAD) — with the vision to enable a data-driven transition of PMI toward a smoke-free future (Table 1). This marked the beginning of a three-year transformation process guided by a data strategy.

3.2.1. *Dual data strategy*

To implement the vision of a data-driven enterprise, PMI decided on a dual data strategy that addresses defense and offense simultaneously. This dual strategy was regarded by PMI as crucial for turning data into business opportunities, while effectively addressing the existing data-related issues and breaking down data silos. It involved two major pillars that complemented each other:

- *Data foundation (defensive aspects of the data strategy),* ensuring trusted and consistent data across the enterprise by defining and controlling data ownership, data policies, data-related principles, and data-related standards across all functions;

- *Analytics delivery (offensive aspects of the data strategy)*, facilitating experimentation with data, design and reuse of algorithms to generate business value by providing actionable insights, and delivery of robust data products enabling insights consumption at scale.

Both pillars were communicated internally using the "carrot-and-stick" metaphor: While Analytics Delivery yields tangible business benefits from data (referred to as "the carrot"), the realization of these benefits for business units is contingent on their simultaneous commitment to work on the Data Foundation (referred to as "the stick").

3.2.2. *Building blocks and roadmap*

Each of the two major pillars was further divided into a set of building blocks, outlining the major areas of activity, with a dedicated team of specialized staff for each:

- *Data Foundation* was subdivided into Data Architecture, Data Management, Data Quality, and Data Engineering.
- *Analytics Delivery* was segmented into Analytics Enablement, Data Science, and Business Intelligence.

The teams were supported by the *Program Management Office* (PMO) and a *Data Protection* team. Data Protection activities were overseen by PMI's information systems and legal teams, external to the EAD organization.

The roadmap for the first three years of PMI's data transformation reflected these building blocks and concretized them with specific objectives. The roadmap underwent regular reviews during quarterly workshops conducted by the EAD team. The objectives were broken down into quarterly targets, which were measured and communicated across the organization to foster transparency regarding the progress achieved. Based on the reported figures, and by incorporating lessons learned, the roadmap was and is continuously adjusted and fine-tuned.

3.2.3. *The three-year transformation*

In the *first phase*, which spanned approximately one and a half years, the priorities were set on establishing the Data Foundation, namely Data Management and Data Architecture, and on attaining initial results from Data Science. During this period, the following outcomes were realized across five building blocks:

In the domain of *Data Management*, company-wide governance structures, processes, and standards were established. This initial phase saw the definition of over 40 data owners and more than 200 business/data experts. It was accompanied by the introduction of a master data management system (SAP MDG) and a data catalog as a data governance platform (Collibra). In the area of *Data Architecture*, conceptual data models were defined in the five central areas of product data, device data, customer data, consumer data, and business partner data. The conceptual model and the semantics were mapped into a logical model, which is system-agnostic, to understand the linkages between data from an enterprise-wide perspective.

To develop *Data Science* from scratch, employees with the corresponding skills were hired and a data lake infrastructure, known as the PMI Data Ocean, was built. Subsequently, these employees spearheaded the implementation of the initial data science use cases. The *Analytics Enablement* team defined and developed the tools and methods for capturing the analytics demand and implemented use cases with the appropriate technology.

The *Project Management Office* (PMO) took over the coordination of activities involved in promoting and communicating data-related activities across the company and set up training programs for data literacy. With the European General Data Protection Regulation (GDPR), *Data Protection* became an additional priority — and building block — in PMI's roadmap. Here, EAD assumed the responsibility of implementing and controlling the global privacy protection (GPP) framework developed by the legal and IS departments for the digital business function.

The *second phase* was focused on substantiating the remaining building blocks, namely *Data Quality* and *Data Engineering*: Data quality activities covered the definition of data quality rules, audits, tools, interventions, and improvements. They were deliberately placed in the second phase as data quality presupposes a certain level of maturity of the data management and the data architecture building blocks. Emphasis was also placed on Data Engineering, encompassing the implementation and operation of data pipelines to onboard data to the Data Ocean and facilitate the delivery of data science as well as BI products. Based on PMI's business priorities, the Data Ocean contained 200+ business-critical datasets, 15+ complex data products, and 30+ data science use cases supported by the DS Labs environment.

In Analytics Delivery, there was a sustained emphasis on *Data Science,* with the expansion of the use cases, supported by *Analytics Enablement.* This was now complemented by the incorporation of *Business Intelligence* to provide operational reporting and ad hoc analysis products to enhance decision-making through descriptive analytics. The technology stack was redesigned to support the purposes of massive BI with SnowFlake, WhereScape, and PowerBI.

3.2.4. *Achievements after three years*

Within three years, PMI made significant progress toward becoming a data-driven company. Initially comprising six members, the EAD team experienced rapid growth, reaching 60 employees within the first year, and surpassing 80 employees by the second year, with expansion to 100 employees within the third year. This workforce allocation is divided, with two-thirds dedicated to analytics delivery and one-third to data foundation activities. EAD's organizational assignment changed several times over the three years:

First, the the Chief Data Officer reported to the Chief Data Officer (CFO), then to commercial business functions, and finally to the IT department under the Chief Technology Officer (CTO) leadership. Although the overall vision and roadmap were maintained, each organizational change introduced adjustments in priorities and mandates. In financial terms, the objective outlined in PMI's data strategy was to generate five times more business value than the costs incurred by EAD. At the end of the third year, data science use cases with a potential of 500 million USD had been identified and were being worked on.

4. Developing and Implementing a Successful Data Strategy

As part of our research in the Competence Center Corporate Data Quality (CC CDQ), we have monitored and analyzed the evolution of data strategies in more than 30 firms spanning various industries and sizes, including the illustrative example presented in the previous section. Although there is no singular approach to creating and implementing a data strategy, we observed key success factors, which we have consolidated into the following set of recommendations.

4.1. *How to Develop a Data Strategy?*

Recommendation 1: Commence the data strategy with a mandate from the top management.
While data and analytics experts often identify issues and advocate for an enterprise-wide data strategy, they are seldom in a position to define one. The development of a data strategy necessitates a clear mandate from the top management. In practical terms, this implies that one or more executive board members act as the sponsor for the data strategy. Alternatively, a board with high-ranking representatives from key business functions should take responsibility for the data strategy as the designated owner.

Recommendation 2: Integrate top-down and bottom-up approaches.
The development of the data strategy must integrate top-down and bottom-up approaches. In the top-down approach, pertinent strategies, such as corporate, digital, and IT strategies, are

reviewed and fed into the data strategy. This involves translating strategic goals and requirements into data-related goals and requirements and subsequently formulating areas of action. In the bottom-up approach, data challenges and use cases from the different business functions or divisions as well as from current strategic initiatives are analyzed. Promising data use cases where data bring tangible business benefits or data-related issues that could yield significant savings if addressed could be identified as a result. Justification for funding the central team must stem from successful data use cases and the resolution of critical data-related issues.

Recommendation 3: Develop a data strategy in close collaboration with business, data, and IT stakeholders.
Data-related responsibilities cannot be "delegated" to a single department but necessitate collaboration among specialists and managers with diverse skill sets and from business, data, and IT. Even though the business functions will ultimately benefit from data, it is crucial to recognize that not all managers and employees are inherently data literate. Therefore, data and analytics teams play a pivotal role in transforming business requirements into data requirements and products. While IT holds responsibility for architecting, delivering, and maintaining the required infrastructure and applications, business development and enterprise architecture groups often serve as facilitators in developing the data strategy.

4.2. *What are the Key Elements of a Data Strategy?*

Recommendation 4: Formulate a compelling vision for the future role of data in business.
A data strategy should inspire and motivate everyone in the organization with a compelling vision for the future role and management of data, emphasizing its business value. Metaphors such as "data as an asset" are often used but need to be made tangible and contextualized for the organization.

Recommendation 5: Address both data monetization and data foundation with a balanced approach.

Defining essential capabilities needed to realize the vision and evolve into a more data-driven company lies at the core of a data strategy. These capabilities must address both data foundation and data monetization in a balanced manner, as demonstrated by the "carrot-and-stick" metaphor in the PMI case study. We recommend a practical approach to derive these capabilities by analyzing identified high-priority data use cases and understanding fundamental issues with the way data are collected, maintained, and used. Capability-building within a data strategy should comprise the following aspects:

- *People, roles, and responsibilities*: Defining the necessary data and analytics roles, committees, their responsibilities, organizational anchoring, and interactions.
- *Processes and methods*: Establishing standards and guidelines for managing and using data consistently across the organization.
- *Data life cycle processes*: Defining the main activities along the life cycle (from creation to archiving) of each data object and data product.
- *Applications*: Providing the necessary functionalities, including data catalogs, master data management, or the different components of the enterprise analytics platform.
- *Data architecture and documentation*: Defining the data model at different levels as well as the storage and distribution of data.
- *Performance management*: Monitoring data quality, availability, and the tangible results of all data-related activities.

Recommendation 6: Define a clear roadmap to guide the transformation process.

A data strategy defines the areas of activity for developing and expanding essential capabilities, while a roadmap guides the transformation process by breaking down activities and objectives.

Typically spanning a period of two to three years, it establishes priorities and a rough timeline, considering available resources and budgets. It is a commendable practice to iteratively review, adjust, and refine the roadmap on a quarterly basis to integrate the ongoing learnings and address the most pressing business needs.

Recommendation 7: Establish clear guidelines and principles for data in the organization's code of conduct.
A code of conduct serves as a tool for setting clear guidelines and principles on how the organization deals with data. It has become a crucial element in the context of growing ethical concerns and stricter data and AI regulations. A data code of conduct establishes cornerstones for the day-to-day handling of data, facilitating operational decisions, fostering a uniform understanding among employees across various locations and units, and serving as the basis for a data-centric culture. Examples of these principles include "Data is a shared asset" (in order to break down silos) or "We collect, process and use data responsibly" (in order to emphasize that data should be handled with decency). The principles can address both employees within the company as well as suppliers and customers outside the company. Companies increasingly make control and ownership of sensitive customer data part of their data strategy. Not only do they adhere to local laws and regulations but they also interpret them more strictly and therefore (over)fulfill the expectations of their customers (data ethics).

4.3. *How to Achieve and Demonstrate Progress?*

Recommendation 8: Leverage the data strategy as a communication tool.
With their data strategy, organizations not only guide the data-related activities company-wide but also instill an understanding of the importance of data and recognizing their business value among employees. Hence, the data strategy should be formulated and presented in a way that is comprehensible for everyone in the

company, recognizing its role not only as a plan but also as a communication tool.

Recommendation 9: Regularly monitor the progress and success of the data strategy and ensure that it is updated.
The implementation of the data strategy must be traceable, with predefined KPIs and target values to measure progress and success. Data strategies are regularly reviewed to assess both their progress in terms of activities and milestones as well as their success measured by business outcomes, such as the monetary value realized by data use cases. Updating the data strategy is recommended every one to three years to ensure it remains aligned with evolving business needs and technological advancements.

5. Conclusion

A data strategy creates a strong and robust enterprise-wide framework, supporting the transformation toward a more data-driven company and unlocking the full business value of data and analytics across the enterprise. If done well, a data strategy fosters synergies between diverse data-related activities and use cases in different parts of the organization, aligns these endeavors with strategic priorities, and ensures investments in critical groundwork that is often overlooked. A data strategy not only guides the transformation through a clear roadmap with priorities and resources but also serves as an advocate for data and their ethical and compliant use, actively supporting the overall transformation process.

The recent technological advancements in the field of generative AI have underscored the importance of having a well-defined and well-implemented data strategy. Companies seeking to craft or revise their data strategy in response to the evolving technologies should leverage the insights and recommendations outlined in this chapter, which synthesize learnings from data strategies in more than 30 firms spanning various industries and sizes.

References

Bean, R. (2021). Why is it so hard to become a data-driven company? *Harvard Business Review Online.* https://hbr.org/2021/02/why-is-it-so-hard-to-become-a-data-driven-company.

Chandler, A. D. (1962). *Strategy and Structure, Chapters in the History of the American Industrial Enterprise.* Washington: Beard Books.

DalleMule, L. and Davenport, T. H. (2017). What's your data strategy? *Harvard Business Review* 95(3), 112–121.

Fadler, M., Legner, C., and Pentek, T. (2020). PMI's Journey towards a Data-Driven Enterprise. CC CDQ Working Report.

Legner, C. and Pentek, T. (2021). *Data Strategy.* CC CDQ eBook.

Legner, C., Pentek, T., and Otto, B. (2020). Accumulating design knowledge with reference models: Insights from 12 years' research into data management. *Journal of the Association of Information Systems,* 21(3), 735–770.

MIT CISR Data Board. (2018). How to create a successful data strategy? https://cisr.mit.edu/reports/create-a-data-strategy.

Rumelt, R. P. (2011). *Good Strategy, Bad Strategy: The Difference and Why It Matters,* 1st edn. New York: Crown Business.

Wixom, B., Beath, C., and Owens, L. (2023). *Data Is Everybody's Business: The Fundamentals of Data Monetization,* MIT Press.

Chapter 3

Unlocking the Power of Data: Key Strategies for Success

Meri Rosich* and Cat Rüst[†]

Board Director & Advisor, Professor of Data and AI Strategy, Former CIO/CDO
[†]*Repeat Tech founder, CRO, Global Head of Tech, Head of Innovation Technologies*

Abstract

This chapter explores how data has emerged as a pivotal change agent, reshaping the contemporary business landscape. Far beyond a mere resource for exploitation like oil, data now actively enables and propels business transformation by expanding its capabilities to extract insights at an unprecedented scale. Further accelerating this data revolution, innovations like AI, IoT sensors, and advanced analytics amplify the business impact of data.

New C-suite roles, like the Chief Data Officer, help enterprises navigate this complex data terrain by bridging strategic acumen with technical data literacy. Meanwhile, organizational structures must shift from rigid silos to fluid, collaborative data teams that can respond quickly to data-driven disruption.

This chapter highlights how data can drive comprehensive change in leadership methods, team interactions, and alignment of business strategy with technology capabilities. In this context, deciding between isolated and collaborative data teams is a fundamental factor that shapes a successful data-driven transformation.

In conclusion, leveraging the tremendous potential of data responsibly presents complex challenges around ethics and governance, which must be navigated for sustainable success.

Keywords: Data-driven strategies, leadership analytics, tech innovation, global team management, data literacy, women in tech, tech impact, sustainable data.

1. Introduction

In the present landscape of constant change, data has matured beyond a mere commodity into a vital force propelling ongoing transformation across sectors. Unlike finite assets such as oil, data actively feeds an exponential cycle of insight unlocking and capability-building that accelerates change dramatically. In this context, traditional banking and fossil fuel giants that once sat at the top of industry power now cede dominance to digitally native innovators like Alphabet, Amazon, Apple, and Grab that essentially wield data as a core strategic asset.

This shift personifies the depth to which data is reshaping enterprises in foundational ways that far transcend superficial change management. Data is rapidly becoming intertwined into the very heart of traditional business models, workflows, and value creation pathways across industries. Meanwhile, a complementary stack of technologies including AI, IoT sensors, cloud engineering, and advanced analytics further amplifies data's business impact by enabling massive collection and enhanced sensemaking capabilities.

Chief Data Officers are emerging as vital, new cross-disciplinary executives able to converse fluently in both business strategy and data science worlds. Their bilingual ability to bridge domains enables insightful navigation of today's turbulent data-centric business terrain. As organizations struggle to harness the latent potential within rapidly proliferating data resources, enterprise architecture has also become increasingly important. More collaborative, team-oriented data structures defeat siloed functions to power innovation and adaptation.

Now recognized as a mission-critical business asset, data enables a wave of transformation spanning far beyond tech to reshape sectors from healthcare to transportation. This also requires a shift beyond reactive adaptation to proactive adoption of a data-centric culture as well as decision automation. Additionally, organizational tensions between isolated knowledge silos and collaborative insight multiplicity need to be resolved effectively. The increasing importance of diverse and adaptable data teams, avoiding rigid hierarchies, is becoming the driver, steering companies' journeys toward data-driven market leadership — diversity in a data team is not solely about demographics but also is about assembling a mix of skill sets, backgrounds, perspectives, and experiences, thereby fostering robust problem-solving, creativity, and innovation, while adaptability within a data team involves a willingness to embrace new technologies, methodologies, and approaches.

2. The Dynamics of Data

Data has evolved into the vital lifeblood energizing ongoing transformations and evolution across sectors. In this changing landscape, fast-moving data wizards like Alphabet, Amazon, Apple, and Grab dominate through intrinsically data-centric business models fine-tuned for speed and adaptability. This groundbreaking shift spotlights data's ascension beyond a mere commodity or production input. Instead, data increasingly operates as an active change agent enabling and catalyzing continuous business model reinvention and workflow transformation. Vastly increased data collection, storage, and analysis capabilities enhance the awareness and responsiveness of businesses. When paired with complementary technologies like AI, IoT sensors, and cloud engineering, this enables sophisticated rapid adaptation.

Across industries, from manufacturing to healthcare, data infiltrates operations, decision loops, and service delivery as it is embedded into business operations and processes, accelerating an inevitable digital transformation. The result is an unprecedented transformation of conventional businesses as their very foundations are reshaped with redefined business models, innovative strategies, and success metrics, all of which are powered by advanced analytics.

General Electric (GE) is a compelling example of this commitment to transformation. A traditional manufacturing conglomerate, it embraced data-driven strategies to revamp its operations and services. GE implemented data analytics extensively in its industrial operations, using sensors and IoT devices to gather real-time data from its machinery. This shift allowed GE to predict maintenance needs, optimize performance, and reduce downtime significantly. Its aircraft engines, power turbines, and healthcare equipment became "smart" by leveraging data analytics to enhance efficiency and reliability.

In healthcare, GE Healthcare utilized data analytics to improve patient outcomes. It implemented advanced imaging technologies that collected and analyzed vast amounts of medical data, aiding in accurate diagnoses and personalized treatment plans. Moreover, it capitalized on data insights to offer predictive maintenance services to its clients, transforming their business model from selling products to providing solutions and services. This shift allowed GE Healthcare to optimize its resources, improve customer satisfaction, and drive revenue growth.

In this context, acting upon data's exponentially growing strategic potential requires sound data governance foundations able to support enterprise-wide coordination. Hence, centralized governance bodies, led by emerging Chief Data Officer roles, focus on constructing versatile data platforms, policies, pipelines, and relational databases to power business-critical decision-making and adaptation. Once democratized across the organizational network into diverse products and functions through APIs and other interfaces, data truly takes the helm in steering enterprises decisively toward their next horizon.

3. Strategies for Maximizing Data Potential

Constructing high-performing data teams in today's disruptive era requires meticulously orchestrating across organizational architecture, assembling the appropriate skill set, and realigning cultures. The emerging Chief Data Officer plays the critical conductor role — fusing business strategy literacy and technical data fluency to unleash coordinated success.

Capital One appointed Rob Alexander as their Chief Information Officer (CIO) and CDO. Alexander's role exemplifies the fusion of business strategy literacy and technical data fluency. He oversaw the integration of data-driven decision-making into Capital One's DNA, leveraging insights to drive business strategy and innovation.

Under Alexander's leadership, Capital One strategically assembled diverse talent, including data scientists, engineers, and analysts, across the organization. This skill assembly ensured a holistic approach to data utilization, from consumer banking to risk management.

The CDO role at Capital One involved realigning the company culture to prioritize data-centricity. This involved not only technological shifts but also fostering a culture of data-driven decision-making at all levels of the organization. Alexander championed data literacy initiatives, ensuring that employees across departments understood the importance of data and could leverage it effectively in their roles.

Through the alignment of organizational architecture, skill assembly, and cultural realignment, Capital One successfully transformed into a data-driven company. This transformation empowered Capital One to offer personalized financial services, make data-backed strategic decisions, mitigate risks effectively, and continuously innovate in a rapidly changing financial landscape.

Structurally, rigid monolithic blocks are shifting toward more adaptable formations. Centralized, collaborative teams concentrate expertise while enabling the sharing of insights more broadly through the organization. Cloud, automation, and mature

API layers enable secure data mobility and accessibility across the broader organizational network.

Beyond purely technical ability, soft skills like situational awareness, emotional intelligence, and creative ingenuity make data insights resonate and spark action. As data complexity grows exponentially, ethics and sound judgment will remain vital complements to even the most advanced algorithmic approaches in harnessing information responsibly.

Transitioning from fragmented data silos demands cultural commitment alongside architectural realignment. Cultivating responsible and effective data practices is a continuous journey demanding critical self-appraisal, a willingness to recognize biases or blind spots, and a focus on fairness with empathy.

The enterprise data function is increasingly becoming more relevant. An ethical base, adaptable structures fostering collaboration, and a blend of specialized skills and versatile abilities together create a winning data team.

The data domain transcends narrow technical silos. Data ecosystems thrive through open collaboration — forging novel connections across diverse disciplines to better mirror problem complexity. Far beyond rote algorithmic literacy, modern data fluency demands a mosaic of complementary strengths spanning both rational and creative aptitudes.

It is much more than simply "finding a data analyst"; it is about building a foundation that can grow as the corporation learns to embrace a data-first approach.

To grow a more diverse and adaptable team, it is important to consider the following:

- *Recruitment strategies*: Actively seek candidates from various backgrounds, educational paths, and industries, valuing skills and potential over traditional qualifications.
- *Inclusive culture*: Foster an environment where diverse opinions are encouraged and where team members feel comfortable expressing their ideas without fear of judgment.

- *Training and development*: Offer continuous learning opportunities, cross-functional training, and support for skill enhancement to ensure teams stay adaptable.
- *Mentorship programs*: Establish mentorship initiatives to facilitate knowledge sharing and skill development among team
  members.
- *Feedback and iteration*: Encourage feedback loops that allow
  for iterative improvements, ensuring the team remains flexible
  and responsive.

As we dig deeper into cultivating expansive capabilities crucial for maximizing data potential, it is imperative to underscore the strategies that drive high-performing data teams. Organizations today must navigate a disruptive era through architecture orchestration, skill assembly, and cultural realignment, all under the pivotal leadership of a Chief Data Officer.

While we explore these capabilities pivotal to effective data practice, it is clear that alongside technological prowess, human-centric strengths like emotional intelligence and creative ingenuity stand tall as crucial facets in making data insights resonate and incite actionable change.

Key expansive capabilities fueling effective data practices include the following:

A. What organizations must implement:

Multi-lens sensemaking: This entails more than just narrow critical thinking or problem-solving; multi-lens sensemaking requires braiding together logical rigor with holistic systems intuition in order to perceive challenging situations from multiple perspectives simultaneously. Seasoned leaders decompose complex scenarios into layers spanning the tangible and intangible, seeking through empathy and pattern recognition to synthesize broad understandings inclusive of cultural contexts, power dynamics, incentives, and the ability to act for various stakeholders. This guidance goes beyond detached analysis to foster breakthroughs backed by moral conviction.

Netflix is exemplary in its approach to multi-lens sensemaking. Within the company, seasoned leaders decompose complex scenarios into layers spanning cultural contexts, power dynamics, and incentives, seeking insights through empathy and pattern recognition. For instance, while strategizing content creation and recommendation algorithms, for this media and entertainment giant, Netflix analyzes data across demographics, viewing habits, and cultural nuances. This holistic approach allows Netflix to create diverse, relevant content that resonates across various audiences, embracing cultural diversity while maximizing viewer engagement.

Virtual team fluidity: Geographically dispersed data contributors collaborating primarily online impose additional challenges in communication, relationship building, and workflow coordination across data projects relative to tightly integrated in-person teams. Savvy program managers counteract these inherent challenges for remote work by promoting psychological safety, cultivating deeper interpersonal connections, and establishing consistent responsive rhythms virtually. Proficient digital tooling for smooth videoconferencing, asynchronous or synchronous activity awareness, decentralized version control, and modular documentation allows fluid remote teams to work together on data initiatives. With trust and aligned vision filling space across remote locations, virtual data teams can achieve productivity benchmarks through adaptable infrastructure that enables transparent coordination.

GitHub, a platform widely known for its collaborative approach to software development, exemplifies virtual team fluidity. Its savvy program managers have established a decentralized version control system and proficient digital tooling that enables smooth asynchronous or synchronous activity awareness. Despite geographically dispersed contributors, GitHub fosters psychological safety, ensuring teams collaborate transparently and efficiently. This approach has led to seamless collaboration among developers worldwide, enabling the platform's growth and innovation.

Communication versatility: Beyond technical accuracy, sharing data insights impactfully requires crafting compelling narratives that promote intuitive understanding, spark further curiosity, and catalyze change across wide audiences. Data-fluent communicators artfully adapt messaging and mediums to resonate with the perspectives of given listeners, making complex relationships tangible through explanatory analogies, vivid data visualizations, and emphasis on relevance for leadership priorities or community outcomes. To convey multilayered findings, versatile data teams fluidly toggle between modalities spanning quantitative graphs, qualitative case studies, interactive media, and purposeful rhetorical framing that bring core revelations into focus through personalized storytelling styles.

The New York Times showcases communication versatility in data storytelling. The media giant effectively crafts compelling narratives, leveraging data insights to resonate with diverse audiences. Through quantitative graphs, interactive media, and purposeful rhetorical framing, it bridges complex data relationships into intuitive understanding. The Times adeptly utilizes data visualization and explanatory analogies to make multifaceted findings accessible and relevant to readers, sparking curiosity and societal impact through personalized storytelling styles.

Computational thinking: While logical thinking represents a key aptitude within data science fields, computational thinking applies such analytical reasoning for operationalizing solutions to multifaceted problems. It complements pure data analysis by providing frameworks for organizing insights and breaking down tangled decisions into coherent, manageable components that translate intent into executable action that is appropriately responsive to dynamic situational realities. Computationally minded data teams systematically map ambiguous challenges into agile data pipeline architectures able to ingest, process, and activate essential signals efficiently while filtering noise via statistical and AI techniques for improved outcomes.

Google embodies computational thinking in its approach to managing vast amounts of data. The company systematically maps complex challenges into agile data architectures, utilizing AI techniques to filter noise and improve outcomes. Google's infrastructure, including systems like Google Search and Google Maps, demonstrates the application of computational thinking in organizing and processing data efficiently, providing users with relevant, personalized information while managing massive datasets.

Focus amidst complexity: Data environments confront analysts daily with seemingly infinite permutations of approaches and considerations woven through multidimensional challenges with tangled interlinkages. Effective data teams focus their efforts on the most important issues within complex systems, instead of spreading themselves too thin or getting distracted by less significant details. Concentrating cognitive resources demands skillfully filtering complexity down to patterns revealing priority needs and capabilities based on the purpose at hand, combined with wisdom to recognize the appropriate cadence between action and reflection in dynamic contexts.

Amazon exemplifies focus amidst complexity by strategically channeling its cognitive resources to address pivotal pressure points. Amidst its diverse operations, Amazon concentrates on identifying patterns within customer behavior and supply chain operations. By concentrating on crucial areas for improvement, such as delivery efficiency and customer experience enhancements, Amazon navigates complexity to drive innovation and continuous improvement within its extensive ecosystem.

B. Attributes that organizations must nurture:
Social–emotional intelligence: At both the individual and collective levels, social–emotional competencies form the foundation of human trust, relationships, and collaboration. Self-awareness of personal emotional patterns, triggers, and biases allows building mental resilience while reading social cues mindfully. Developing empathy involves earnestly striving to comprehend life experiences fundamentally distinct from one's own, such as the ongoing struggles of those facing adversity and lack of privilege. Through authentic vulnerability, compassion, and moral purpose, data leaders open channels enabling candid idea exchange and psychological safety

across teams tackling data-driven challenges in order to reach shared truths.

Salesforce emphasizes social–emotional intelligence in its approach to fostering team dynamics. The company prioritizes psychological safety and open communication among employees. Salesforce's culture promotes authenticity and compassion, encouraging teams to collaborate candidly while addressing data-driven challenges. Through initiatives like mindfulness workshops and inclusive leadership training, Salesforce nurtures a work environment that values emotional intelligence and supports the mental well-being of its employees.

Adaptive cognition balanced with moral compass: Operating amidst constant volatility, complexity, and uncertainty with finite cognitive resources requires fluidly toggling between focused attention and creative diffusion across complex data problems with many interdependencies. Thought leaders purposefully shift group perspectives between detail-conscious deliberation and expansive brainstorming modes to broaden consideration of alternative actions. Clear guiding principles and ethical considerations answer critical questions on how to validate information sources, weigh uncertain risks versus benefits of potential data uses for different parties, provide a voice to affected groups, and fairly judge appropriate dilemmas as they arise in practice.

Microsoft demonstrates adaptive cognition and a strong moral compass in handling complex data problems. The company purposefully navigates between focused attention and creative diffusion, exploring diverse perspectives on data ethics and responsible AI. Microsoft actively engages in ethical considerations, balancing risks and benefits while providing a voice to affected communities. Initiatives like the AI for Good program reflect its commitment to using technology responsibly for societal benefit.

Cultural competence and humility: Real cultural skill involves more than just basic diversity efforts or forcing people to fit in. It means including different people, methods, and ways of thinking fairly, through honest teamwork across cultures. Striving for cultural competence in approaches to complex data challenges grounded in humanity involves not only building awareness of the lived realities shaping various cultural perspectives but also cultivating an orientation toward lifelong learning based on humility regarding one's inevitable cultural blind spots as an outsider to most subcultures. Modeling sincere curiosity to understand unfamiliar worldviews and data interpretations forges bonds of positive shared purpose across diverse teams pursuing data-driven innovation.

Unilever exhibits cultural competence and humility by embracing diverse perspectives in its data-driven strategies. The company's approach to consumer insights and product development considers cultural nuances and diverse market needs. Unilever's commitment to understanding and respecting various cultural perspectives and local preferences allows it to create products and campaigns that resonate with a global audience while respecting local contexts.

Creative ingenuity: Beyond purely logical cognition, creative aptitudes enable the discovery of solutions to sticky data-centered problems that may seem intractable based on pattern recognition or brute analytical force alone. Creative thought leaders immersed in the data context spark fresher possibilities by intuitively sensing hidden connections, deliberately reframing orthodoxies, and recombining disparate concepts to design novel data architectures and analytics techniques optimized for the situation at hand. Unbound from the constraints of popular existing methods designed for general applicability rather than targeted needs, bespoke solutions manifest that can powerfully magnify the impact of data resources when applied judiciously.

Tesla embodies creative ingenuity in its innovative approach to data-driven solutions in the automotive industry. Beyond logical cognition, Tesla's leaders integrate creative thought into designing novel data architectures and analytics techniques for optimizing vehicle performance and autonomous driving. Their innovative use of data for features like over-the-air updates and self-driving technology reflects a creative mindset, pushing the boundaries of what is possible in the automotive sector.

Transdisciplinarity: No single field holds a monopoly on wisdom for navigating intricate modern challenges tangled with data-driven advances and ethical dilemmas. Assembling diverse expertise across data science, social sciences, humanities, and creative arts as well as affected communities enriches solution finding by exposing blind spots and amalgamating complementary strengths. Transdisciplinary collaboration empowers breakthrough innovations at the intersections of disciplines ranging from combinatorics to ethics. It further enables constructing more complete mental maps incorporating technical and humanistic insights alike when evaluating data initiatives and governance structures for collective benefit.

MIT Media Lab epitomizes transdisciplinarity in its collaborative approach to research. Bringing together experts from diverse fields like data science, social sciences, creative arts, and technology, the lab pioneers innovative solutions at the intersection of disciplines. Projects at the Media Lab, ranging from human–computer interaction to ethical AI, harness the strengths of diverse expertise, fostering breakthroughs by amalgamating technical and humanistic insights for societal impact.

Together, this composite skill set empowers enterprises to translate raw data into responsible and impactful business outcomes efficiently.

As data volumes explode, enterprises recognize the limits of manual analysis. However, advanced analytics now provide a scalable lens to analyze vast datasets. Descriptive stats give way to predictive, then prescriptive algorithms. Eventually, machine learning can semi-autonomously surface valuable signals.

Yet keeping such augmentation ethically anchored remains imperative, not inevitable. All tools reflect embedded priorities and beliefs. To build an ethical data culture, companies need to look beyond just technical abilities. They must examine the motivations, attitudes, and definitions of success that shape their data systems.

Mature data organizations progress across a spectrum — from compliance-focused and siloed toward integrated and open — ultimately infusing the ethos of accountability into everyday behaviors company-wide. Continual transparency, fairness, and truth-seeking become guiding stars orienting data efforts toward positive external impacts aligned with internal values.

Through meticulous cultural nurturing and structure that balance empowered individuals with technical mastery and virtuous intent, the data-powered enterprise reaches a crescendo. When ethics and skill come together, it creates opportunities for everyone.

4. Case Studies and Practical Applications

Across sectors, data is actively enabling the development of improved products, services, and processes as demonstrated in the following examples.

Construction industry transformation: In the construction industry, data analytics stands as a catalyst for significant advancements in efficiency, safety, and precision. Its implementation offers comprehensive insights into operations, introducing augmented reality guidance that remarkably reduces risks while elevating quality, sustainability, and reliability across workflows. Through detailed analytics, construction companies optimize resource allocation, identify potential hazards, and streamline project management. Augmented reality tools enhance on-site decision-making, aiding in accurate planning, design visualization, and real-time monitoring, ultimately revolutionizing traditional construction practices.

Empowering construction integrity: *Screening Eagle Technologies* provides cutting-edge sensor and software solutions tailored for construction stakeholders. Its innovative ecosystem supports the visualization and, eventually, the assessment of the structural integrity of buildings, bridges, dams, and tunnels, while mapping underground utilities. This comprehensive insight empowers asset owners to proactively ensure safety, durability, and environmental sustainability while minimizing remediation costs and optimizing project life cycles.

Augmented reality in design and planning: Companies like *Trimble* have developed AR solutions that overlay digital models onto physical construction sites. Architects and engineers use AR headsets to visualize how designs will integrate into existing structures or landscapes. This technology enables more accurate planning, reducing errors in construction and optimizing resource utilization.

Technology sector evolution: Within the dynamic tech landscape, data remains the cornerstone driving exponential progress. The influence of data extends into every facet of operations, actively fueling product innovation, bolstering business growth, and cementing market leadership. Leveraging consumer data enables personalized experiences, while strategic decision-making relies on data-derived insights, shaping future product scopes. Data-centric initiatives continuously refine tech offerings, ensuring they align with evolving consumer demands and market trends, propelling companies toward sustained relevance and competitive advantage.

Personalization through data analytics: E-commerce giants like *Amazon* leverage sophisticated data analytics to personalize customer experiences. By analyzing past purchase behavior, browsing history, and demographic data, Amazon tailors product recommendations and marketing strategies for individual users. This data-driven personalization enhances customer satisfaction and drives sales.

Data-informed product development: *Google* harnesses user data from various applications to refine its product offerings. Analytics from Google Maps, Gmail, and Search inform feature updates and new product launches. For instance, location data from Maps aids in improving route recommendations, while user feedback shapes Gmail's interface updates, ensuring user-centric design decisions.

Financial services domain advancements: Data in the financial services sector transcends growth facilitation to become the driver for sophisticated risk quantification and mitigation. Advanced analytics transform raw data into actionable intelligence, enabling informed decision-making while instilling trust through client-centricity. The responsible use of data not only supports financial stability but also rebuilds trust by prioritizing client needs, laying a robust foundation for sustainable growth and long-term partnerships.

Risk assessment through machine learning: *JP Morgan Chase* employs machine learning algorithms to assess credit risk. These algorithms analyze vast amounts of data, including transaction history, spending patterns, and economic indicators. This approach enhances risk assessment accuracy, allowing the bank to offer more tailored financial products and lending decisions.

Customer-centric banking solutions: *Bank of America* uses data analytics to understand customer behavior and preferences. By analyzing transaction data and user interactions with digital platforms, it develops personalized banking solutions. For example, predictive analytics help anticipate customer needs, offering timely advice or suggesting suitable financial products.

As data permeates strategy, the nature of competition also evolves. Capability enhancement now interlinks with ethical considerations around privacy, transparency, and bias mitigation built into data practice through governance and culture. While complex challenges endure, proactive investment to align data systems with societal benefits can unlock abundant positive potential.

5. Conclusion

In the dynamic landscape of business, data stands tall as the catalyst driving monumental change across sectors. Data has evolved from a mere commodity to a strategic force reshaping industries, fueling innovation, and redefining success metrics.

This evolution has heralded a pivotal shift in industry dominance. Once-powerful entities in banking and fossil fuels are yielding ground to digitally native innovators like Alphabet, Amazon, Apple, and Grab. These companies leverage and wield data as a core strategic asset to drive business models fine-tuned for speed and adaptability.

Data's metamorphosis from passive input to an active change agent is evident. Data does not just inform decisions; it catalyzes continuous reinvention and workflow transformation. The union of data with advanced technologies like AI, IoT sensors, and cloud engineering amplifies the impact, enabling rapid adaptation across various industries.

Consider GE, a traditional manufacturing conglomerate. By embracing data-driven strategies, it revolutionized operations and services. Predictive maintenance, driven by data analytics from IoT devices, optimized performance and reduced downtime significantly. GE's foray into healthcare involved advanced imaging technologies that improved patient outcomes through accurate diagnoses and personalized treatment plans. This transformation showcases how data integration can redefine business models and create new avenues for value.

Chief Data Officers (CDOs) emerge as pivotal figures. Their bilingual prowess in both business strategy and data science enables insightful navigation in today's data-centric terrain. As organizations strive to harness the latent potential within data resources, enterprise architecture becomes crucial. Collaborative data structures power innovation and adaptation, defeating siloed functions.

Constructing high-performing data teams in this disruptive era requires meticulous orchestration across organizational architecture, skill assembly, and cultural realignment — a marriage of business strategy literacy with technical data fluency. Through holistic talent assembly and culture prioritization, it is possible to transform into a data-driven company, offering personalized services, making data-backed decisions, and innovating continuously.

Adaptable team structures replace rigid monoliths. Cloud, automation, and mature API layers ensure secure data mobility across organizational networks. However, beyond technical prowess, human strengths like emotional intelligence and creative ingenuity are vital. They make data insights resonate, navigating complexity effectively.

Maximizing data potential demands a composite skill set. Multilens sensemaking, virtual team fluidity, communication versatility, computational thinking, and focus amidst complexity form the bedrock. Alongside these skills, social–emotional intelligence, adaptive cognition, cultural competence, creative ingenuity, and transdisciplinarity are essential attributes.

Ethical data use becomes a priority. As advanced analytics offer scalable lenses into vast datasets, maintaining ethical anchors is imperative. Companies must foster an ethical data culture, continually emphasizing transparency, fairness, and truth-seeking.

Data transforms industries. In construction, analytics drive efficiency and safety, introducing augmented reality guidance and optimizing resource allocation. The tech sector thrives on data-driven insights, enabling personalized experiences and refining offerings. Financial services leverage advanced analytics for risk assessment and client-centricity.

The evolving nature of competition revolves around capability enhancement and ethical considerations. Aligning data systems with societal benefits unlocks data's abundant positive potential across industries. In this era of rapid change, responsible data use propels not only business success but also societal advancement.

Chapter 4

Challenges and Best Practices Associated with Data Quality and Acceptable Use of Data

Ram Kumar

Cigna International Health, Dubai, United Arab Emirates
ram.kumar@cignahealthcare.com

Abstract

Data quality and data privacy-related issues and challenges continue to be a key topic for senior executives in organizations as they expose the organization to business risks that could materialize. The issues often lurk behind the scenes until discovered or exposed. With the maturity of data analytics and the artificial intelligence (AI) field, data quality and acceptable use of data from ethical, privacy, and legal perspectives are becoming more critical for organizations. In this chapter, we will discuss some of the best practices associated with data quality and acceptable use of data that organizations have adopted.

Keywords: Data quality, data culture, acceptable use of data, data ethics, data privacy, data strategy, data governance, data management.

1. Introduction

Data are the lifeblood of any organization and form its competitive and strategic asset. In the case of customer-focused organizations, in particular, the increasing importance of acceptable use of data is shining the spotlight on data quality and data governance, raising new questions about the value of data initiatives and who, ultimately, is responsible for their success. Identifying, classifying, and documenting personal information, both internal and external, are critical to managing the acceptable use of data. One example is the GDPR requirement of data validation, which states that businesses are obligated to correct inaccurate or incomplete personal data. Yet many organizations overlook the importance of data validation. Data quality measures the completeness, accuracy, and timeliness of organization data. It is imperative because without comprehensive data quality controls, organizations cannot locate and resolve inaccuracies around personal data.

However, while data quality is critical, simply resolving data quality issues will not guarantee acceptable use and achieve compliance. Instead, organizations must eliminate all siloed data tasks by integrating data quality efforts with data governance. Data quality and acceptable use of data are two essential aspects of monitoring and evaluation that can sometimes pose challenges and trade-offs. How can you ensure that your data collection, analysis, and reporting are accurate, reliable, and useful, while also protecting the rights and dignity of your data subjects, partners, and stakeholders?

In this chapter, we will explore some of the best practices associated with data quality and the acceptable use of data to effectively manage data-related risks to organizations.

2. Data Quality — An Introduction

Imagine what it would be like if every decision was based upon quality, up-to-date information, where everyone trusts the data they use. What would it be like if everyone who uses the data consistently understands the meaning of data, where decisions can be taken faster than ever before? And imagine if the relevant information you need is easily available in a timely manner and need not be hunted down. You are imagining a world that has recognized the value of information/data management. Data are the lifeblood of an organization that drive competition, innovation, and disruption. Data are the foundation for any business operation, analytics, or AI work. An organization may have the best people, best processes, state-of-the-art technology ecosystem, and the best analytical and AI solutions. But if the underlying data that are used by people, processes, technology, and solutions are poor in terms of quality, the outcome produced by people, processes, technology, and solutions will be poor (Kumar and Mani, 1994).

A data quality issue refers to the presence of an intolerable defect in a dataset, such that it reduces the reliability and trustworthiness of the data. Whether a defect is intolerable or not is usually decided upon by the business and that is dependent upon its business risk appetite. For example, data fill rates are a data quality dimension, and the defect rate of that dimension is dependent on the subject area. If a client manager's role is to reach out to clients constantly to understand the quality of service, the client data fill rate should be close to 100% to be considered of high quality allowing the client manager to reach the client through various channels. Common root causes of data quality issues include human errors during data entry like typos or missing values, technical errors like system failures or bugs, process errors such as lack of validation or standardization when capturing or processing data, data transformation errors, data migration errors, data storage and accessibility issues, data governance issues, inconsistent data formats, and environmental errors such as changes in data sources or regulations.

With so much attention and focus on AI in recent times, it is important to understand that if the data used to train an AI model are inaccurate, incomplete, inconsistent, or biased, predictions and decisions based on these models will also be unreliable. High-quality data result in AI systems that are able to make more accurate predictions, provide relevant recommendations, and effectively automate processes. To summarize, the quality of data-driven outcomes of any kind is directly proportional to the quality of the data that are used to produce the outcomes. There is no silver bullet that would fix data quality. It requires a combination of people, processes, technology, and importantly the right culture in the organization to address it.

3. Data Quality Best Practices

Many organizations approach data quality issues by applying a project lens, i.e., fixing data quality issues by creating a project. This is a short-term thinking mindset. Data quality management is an ongoing process with no end date as organizations are required to continuously measure, monitor, and manage data quality. Obviously, how exactly this can be managed is a challenge confronting senior executives. Until recent times, organizations in general did not prioritize data quality and there was a general assumption that implementing a technology solution will fix data quality. However, the failures of many IT, digital analytics, and AI projects due to poor-quality data has started to change the mindset of organizations. Data quality is not a technology or process problem. It is a people problem as people are the ones who implement technology and operational solutions. This calls for a "data quality by design" culture at the organizational level. Since this has to do with changing people's mindsets, data quality by design is a cultural transformation journey that requires people at all levels in the organization to embrace the change.

3.1. *Organization Priority*

This is the most critical requirement to drive data quality best practices in an organization. Data quality is an organizational problem and not an IT or operational problem. Every employee who uses data should be responsible for its quality. If only half of the company is committed to ensuring data quality, then you can expect no better than 50% of the data to be of good quality. All stakeholders must understand and take responsibility for data quality.

To get organizational buy-in, data quality must be supported and promoted at every level of management, including the C-suite. If executives and business leaders do not prioritize data and data quality, data managers, business managers, operations managers, and IT managers will not either.

3.2. *Develop a Data Quality Management Framework*

It is important for an organization to have a well-defined data quality framework as part of its data strategy. The goal of the framework is to aid strategic planning and help build a roadmap to drive initiatives for data quality. The framework assigns accountability for the quality of an information asset that resides within the business, supported by holistic, informative, and reliable data quality processes, empowered owners, and measures and metrics linked to performance management and KPIs. Figure 1 is an example of a comprehensive data quality framework (Kumar, 2011).

The framework is comprehensive and has a number of elements supporting data quality best practices. The framework is made up of four key components:

- **Data quality benchmark:** The first step is to define what data quality means for your organization and what criteria you will use to assess it. The next step is to assess your current data quality maturity level, based on your data quality goals and criteria. You can use a data quality maturity model, such as the Gartner or the CMMI, to evaluate your data quality capabilities and practices. A data quality maturity model can help you identify your strengths and weaknesses and provide you with a roadmap for improvement. The roadmap can focus on quick wins and build maturity incrementally leading up to value creation. The third step is to benchmark your data quality maturity against your peers and industry standards to see how you

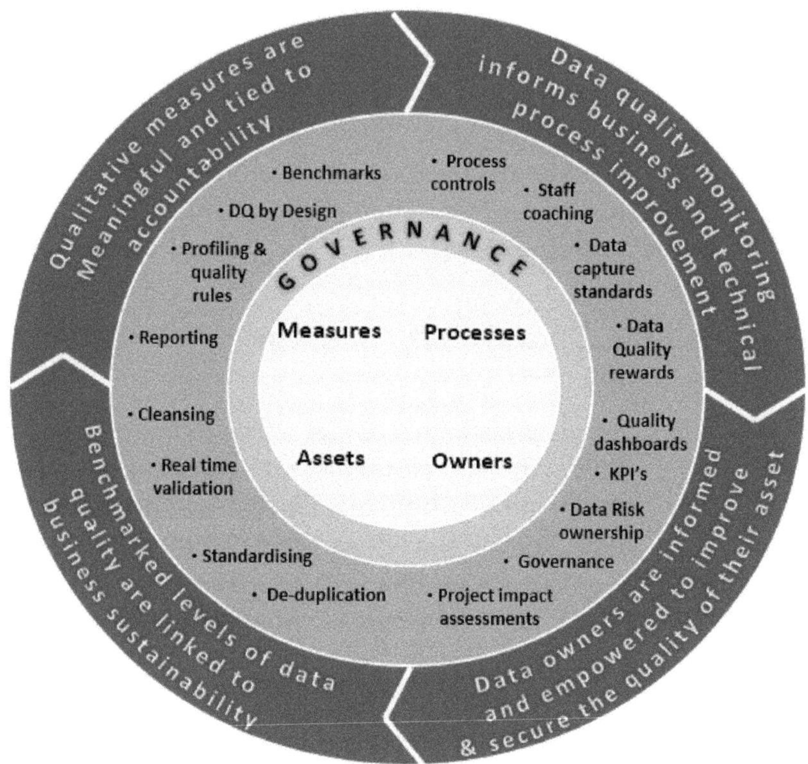

Fig. 1. Data quality framework.

compare, identify areas where you can learn from others, and set a target in terms of where you want to be. You can use various sources of information and data to benchmark your data quality maturity, such as industry reports, surveys, case studies, and best practices. The fourth step is to analyze the gaps and opportunities for improvement, based on your data quality maturity assessment and benchmarking results. You can use a SWOT analysis, a gap analysis, or a root cause analysis to identify and prioritize the areas where you need to improve your data quality and the factors that enable or hinder your data quality improvement.

- **Data quality measures, monitoring and reporting:** Once you have done the benchmarking, identified areas for improvement, and implemented measures to plug the gaps, it is important to measure, monitor, and communicate your data quality maturity progress and results to ensure that you are on track and that you are delivering value to your organization and stakeholders. You can use data quality metrics, dashboards, reports, and feedback mechanisms to track and evaluate your data quality improvement efforts and outcomes. You can also use data quality stories, testimonials, and awards to showcase and celebrate your data quality achievements and best practices.

- **Data quality governance:** Data quality is an important pillar in the data governance framework and plays a vital role in an organization's ability to meet established governance standards. While both exist as individual models, effective implementation of data quality and data governance structures has the potential to produce a symbiotic system that ultimately upholds an organization's strategic goals and informs decision-making. The principal difference between data governance and data quality is that data governance provides oversight of and management for an organization's information, whereas data quality is focused on the integrity and value of the information itself. These two forces possess their own intricacies, but organizations have an opportunity to capitalize on their multifaceted nature to build complementary data quality and data governance structures that help meet their goals. Data quality monitoring is a component of data governance from the data management perspective. Compliance is one of the areas in which data governance and data quality intersect. Take the healthcare or education sectors as examples: Both have regulations that delineate rights to information and how the data can be accessed and shared. In healthcare in the USA, HIPAA protects patient information; in education, the Family Educational Rights and Privacy Act protects student information. A comprehensive data governance plan should reference governing regulations that detail requirements for managing an organization's unique data storage, privacy, and security requirements. To complement these regulatory needs, data quality systems should be designed to monitor information that an organization is required to safeguard or report back to a regulatory entity. This same information should be monitored for completeness, timeliness, accuracy, and validity to ensure compliance with the regulations. The data quality dimensions should support the governance standard.

- **Drive data quality by design culture:** Data quality by design is a method used in any software application, business process development, or analytical or AI solution development to address data quality up front. It involves understanding the quality of critical data elements and design features as well as designing functions and processes that ensure high-quality data are captured right from the conceptualization stage of the project. This can be as simple as having no free format text while capturing data or having data validation rules in online forms, or something more complex such as validating mobile numbers through SMS acknowledgment. Data quality should not be an afterthought, and this avoids having to clean up data as a one-off project. Data quality by design processes should be implemented as part of the software development or analytical and AI solution development life cycle. The following is a global best-practice case study (Kumar, 2011) in which a company implemented the following strategies to drive the data quality culture across the organization:
  - **Accountability from the top:** An enterprise's data strategy to promote data-driven culture and value creation requires support from the top, namely, the CEO and his/her team, and this is critical. They should lead from the front and by example to drive cultural change. A bottom-up approach is not sustainable. The CEO and the board of an organization took ownership of driving data culture in the organization. This was well supported by other layers of the organization. The board and CEO were very clear that it was not

about "Sponsorship," but "Accountability and Ownership." A CEO can sponsor many initiatives, but not necessarily be accountable for the outcomes. The CEO in question took accountability as the "Data Champion" of the organization by walking the talk.

The data strategy and execution team directly reported to the CEO to drive the culture. The following were key guiding foundational statements that they agreed upon to develop and execute the data strategy:

- ○ Get the right data to the right place at the right time in the right format with the right quality in the right context and with the right security.
- ○ Democratize data by ensuring that the data assets flow seamlessly, interoperate across the organization's business processes and technology systems, and reach the hands of the users with minimum effort, and
- ○ Business functions, business processes, supporting organizational structures, and technologies will be developed and managed around data strategy by putting "data at the center" of the organization.

- **Performance KPIs to drive data culture:** Data culture-related KPIs were implemented for all employees across the organization as part of their balance scorecard that measured their performance. This meant that a specific percent of the CEO and senior leadership team's annual bonus was tied to these KPIs. The senior leadership led by example and furthered the drive toward a data quality culture. Figure 2 shows the implementation of the performance KPIs. A few examples of KPIs include a data quality measure of critical data elements (e.g., customer data), a data literacy penetration rate, data risk management, and the accuracy of data-driven insights used for decision-making.
- **Comprehensive data literacy program:** All employees of the organization (new joiners or existing) across all levels irrespective of their designation, and with no exceptions, had to undergo a comprehensive data literacy program to

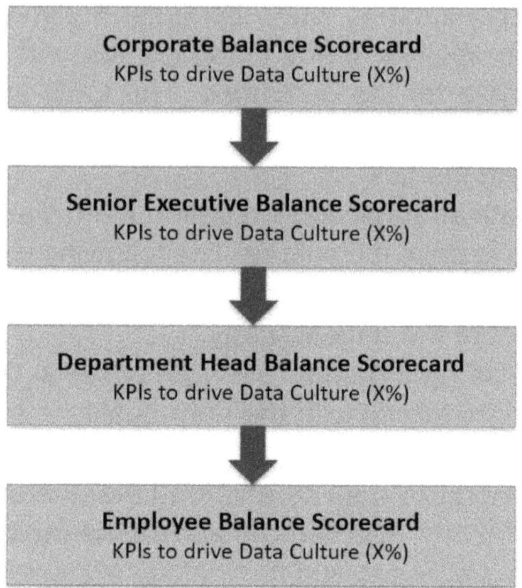

Fig. 2.   Implementation of KPIs to drive data culture.

help them understand the foundations of data management and use across the data life cycle, and the value of data to the business as part of an "Employee Training Program." This was mandated as an annual training program.

- **Minimum data standards framework:** Comprehensive and clear data principles, policies, standards, and procedures with supporting practical data governance frameworks were developed and executed as part of the data strategy and implemented across the organization. Any initiatives including technology and business processes had to comply with these "minimum standards." The implementation was regularly audited for compliance.
- **Data-driven technology solutions:** All technology and operational solutions were built/transformed based on the data strategy. A comprehensive enterprise architecture approach was used to build technology solutions and supporting processes so that changes in the future could be well managed from an impact perspective. The enterprise

architecture was regarded as the "Blueprint of the Organization." This consisted of the business architecture, data architecture, integration architecture, infrastructure architecture, solution architecture, and security architecture components supporting the data strategy. Data architecture was seen as the bridge/common denominator between business and technology. Core foundational data components were implemented based on which technology solutions were developed. Today's technology is tomorrow's legacy, processes change, and people move on. But this is not the case with data assets. They continue to add value. Therefore, ensuring that foundational data components are implemented was critical. Some of the key components implemented include master data management, data governance, data security by design, and data quality by design. Data quality by design was introduced at the conceptual phase of any technology, operation, or business issue.

- **Comprehensive data quality program:** The quality of data-driven business outcomes or decision-making is directly proportional to the quality of the data used, and data quality is a business problem and not a technology problem. The organization implemented a "Data Quality by Design" culture, with the following key initiatives:
  - *Data quality branded*: Data quality was branded with an icon called "DeeKew" (Fig. 3) which served as the

Fig. 3.   DeeKew, organization's data quality mascot.

mascot of the organization. All data quality-related initiatives (internal or external) were organized under the brand. This brand was a reflection of how serious the organization was about data quality, and it was used to remind all the employees about the importance of data quality.

- *Measure data quality*: Data quality was measured, validated, and monitored at the point of data entry by employees (e.g., branches and call center employees) and technology applications against a set of data quality dimensions. Data quality dashboards with supporting processes were created to regularly monitor the health of data, and many initiatives to improve data quality were implemented. Five data quality dimensions were measured and monitored: completeness, validity, accuracy, timeliness, and frequency.
- *Data quality rewards for employees*: Data captured or entered by employees located at the branches or call centers were measured and monitored against the data quality dimensions and employees were rewarded accordingly. The reward was generally given as cash. This motivated the employees to focus on data quality.
- *Data quality award*: All branches capturing and entering data were measured for data quality and the best-performing branch for the month and its members were rewarded with a trophy and individual awards. The worst- and best-performing branches were named in the organization's intranet portal.
- *Annual data quality award*: During the organization's annual day celebrations, the CEO recognized and presented a "Data Quality Branch of the Year" award to the best-performing branch for the year from the data quality perspective.
- *Data quality discount program for customers*: For customers providing quality data (e.g., valid email address, mobile number, and address), discounts on the premiums

they pay were introduced. Capturing accurate customer data helped the organization serve the customers better.

- ○ *Data quality discount program for brokers*: Brokers tend to hold on to their customer details and do not generally provide quality customer data. For brokers providing quality customer data, better commissions were provided.
- ○ *Communication on data quality*: The CEO led from the front by regularly sending newsletters and email communications to all employees from his desk on the importance and role of data strategy and data quality to the organization.
- ○ *Data quality KPI:* Data quality was implemented as a key KPI in the organization's risk profile that was a subject of discussion at the board level.

4. Acceptable Use of Data

We will discuss some best practices around acceptable use of data, which is critical for any organization in managing data-related risks. Gaps in managing the risks may result in reputational damage, loss of customers, and penalties. Calculating data risks is the first and most crucial activity in data risk management and helps define the classification and controls that enable the management of ongoing data risk. It is important to ensure that the risks associated with data across their life cycle are managed effectively and efficiently.

Acceptable use of data refers to the ethical, privacy, and legal principles governing how data should be collected, classified, processed, shared, stored, and retained/destroyed. It encompasses a range of guidelines and practices that help ensure that data are handled responsibly and in a manner that respects individual privacy, complies with applicable laws and regulations, and maintains trust and integrity in an organization. *To an* organization, having access to customer data is a privilege given by customers, *as customers* trust that the organization will ensure their data are protected from abuse and are used wisely in a transparent manner.

In the evolving field of data science, analytics, and AI, the ethical use of data is a critical subject. The ethical use of data and data-driven algorithms involve doing the right thing in the design, functionality, and use of data in AI and analytics. It involves evaluating how data are used and what they are used for, who does and should have access, and anticipating how data could be misused. It means thinking through which data should and should not relate to other data and how to securely store, move, and use data. Ethical use considerations include privacy, bias, access, personally identifiable information, encryption, legal requirements, and restrictions, and what might go wrong.

AI and analytical solutions are responsible for making predictions, classifications, and decisions that will affect individuals and societies. These solutions have the potential to be a great tool for eliminating bias and discrimination, but they can also cause it. The influence of these solutions on decision-making is growing at an unprecedented rate. But what happens when these solutions make a mistake? Or worse, what happens when the solutions operate with inherent biases in the data or the programs written by individuals? The goal of AI and analytical solutions is to make decisions that are as objective as possible and without any biases. However, this is not always possible. Bias is a problem because machines are not able to understand the nuances of human language and behavior.

5. Acceptable Use of Data Best Practices

Having best practices in organizations to manage the use of data is not only a legal requirement in many jurisdictions but also an essential aspect of building trust, credibility, and positive reputation with individuals and society by ensuring that data are used in a responsible and ethical manner. The following are some of the key best practices followed by organizations that have been successful in implementing acceptable use of data policies.

5.1. *Be Clear With Your Position Regarding Acceptable Use of Data*

It is important to have a clear position in your organization when it comes to acceptable use of data, i.e., finding the right balance between acceptable use of data and data monetization or data-driven innovation. The difference between doing right and doing what various people (e.g., customers, community) think is right is significant. An organization acts responsibly when it is concerned both with handling data in a way that aligns with its values and with being perceived by others as handling data in such a manner. Balancing these two non-equivalent concerns should be a priority.

An organization should understand that information has value that can be extracted and turned into new products and services, and this is where ethics comes into play. The degree to which ethics plays a role in this process is, of course, more complicated than a simple identification of which information is "ancillary" and which is not. The ethical impact is highly context dependent. But to ignore the ethical impact is to court an imbalance between the benefits of innovation and the detriments of risk. Failing to evaluate the ethical impacts of the data collected from its customers and yet using the data would lead to the risk of damaging relationships with customers, exposing the organization to the risks of unintended consequences. Ethical evaluation should include both an understanding of how the organization will utilize the customer data that describe an enormously wide variety of historical actions, characteristics, and behaviors (data-handling practices) and an understanding of the core values that the organization holds.

A best-practice approach is to utilize the acceptable use of the data framework (Kumar, 2015) as shown in Fig. 4 to identify risks and make informed decisions before the organization delivers any of its data products or data services for consumption by its customers, partners, and third parties. The goal of this approach is to develop a capacity to incorporate ethical inquiry into the

                                R. Kumar

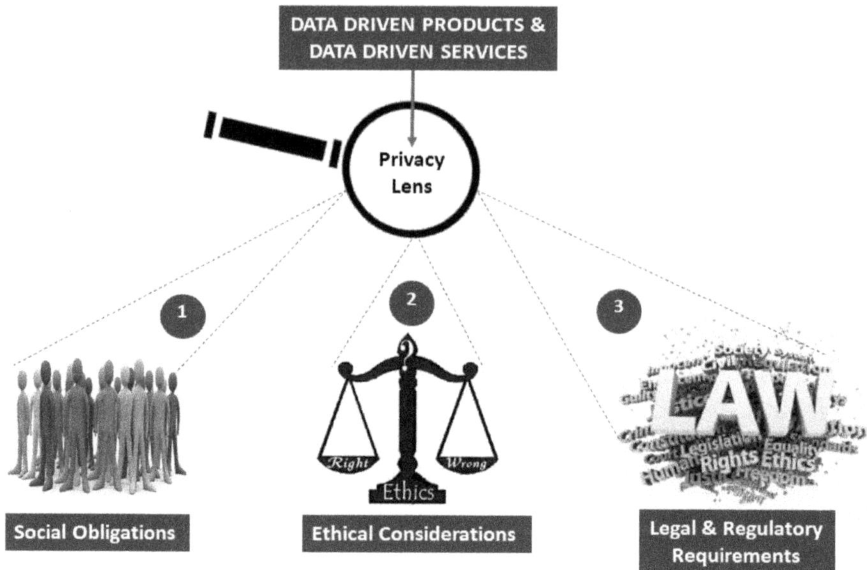

Fig. 4.   An approach to acceptable use of data.

organization's normal course of doing business. An inquiry is a way of talking about the organization's values in the context of the actions that the organization would take in relation to the opportunities that data provide. Learning to recognize and actively engage ethical decision points is one way to start building that capability.

The strategic value of taking a leadership role in driving the alignment of ethical values and action has benefits both internally and externally, which include the following:

- Faster consumer adoption by reducing fear of the unknown (by answering customer questions such as, "How are you using my data?").
- Reduction of friction from legislation due to a more thorough understanding of constraints and requirements.
- Increased pace of innovation and collaboration derived from a sense of purpose generated by explicitly shared values.

- Reduction in risk of unintended consequences from an overt consideration of long-term, far-reaching implications of the use of big-data technologies
- Social good generated from leading by example.

Topics and vocabulary that often arise during ethical decision points include the following:

- **Intention:** The intentions of those who through direct or surreptitious means have access to the data in question.
- **Security:** The security of the data in the hands of each entity in the data chain.
- **Likelihood:** The probability that access to specific data would result in either benefit or harm.
- **Aggregation:** The mixture of possibilities derived from correlating available data.
- **Responsibility:** The various degrees of obligation that arise at each point in the data chain.
- **Identity:** The single or multiple facets of characteristic descriptions that allow an individual to be uniquely individuated.
- **Ownership:** The status of who holds what usage rights at each point in the data life cycle.
- **Reputation:** The judgment(s) that may be derived from available data.
- **Benefit:** The specific contribution or value the available data are expected to make.
- **Harm:** The sort of harm that might come from access to specific data.

To ensure that data are used in the right way for any analytics or AI initiatives, or as a matter of fact, for any initiatives using customer data, applying the acceptable use of data framework helps determine whether the use falls within the principles and risk parameters set by the organization.

6. Summary

By balancing data quality and acceptable use of data in an organization, the organization can not only meet its legal and ethical obligations but also maximize the value and impact of its data. Enhancing the credibility, reliability, and usefulness of the organization's data can support evidence-based decision-making and learning. Additionally, balancing data quality and acceptable use of data can help an organization build trust, credibility, respect, and collaboration with its partners, customers, stakeholders, and shareholders, as well as reduce the risks of errors, gaps, biases, breaches, or misuse. Furthermore, demonstrating accountability and transparency in the organization's work can contribute to the advancement of data ethics in the sector in which the organization operates.

References

Kumar, V. R. (2015). Leading your organization into the data driven future. In: *Future Enterprise 2015 Conference*, Sydney, Australia, June 2015.

Kumar, R. and Mani, N. (1994). Learning to control dynamic systems. In: *Proceedings of IEEE International Conference on Systems, Man and Cybernatics*, Texas, USA, October, 1994.

Chapter 5

Personal Data Privacy, Industry Data Regulations, and Data Security — Three Sides of the Same Coin

Terry Ray

Imperva, a Thales Company, Austin, USA
terry.ray@thalesgroup.com

Abstract

Using, storing, and sharing private data are necessary parts of doing business even while those data remain highly governed by regulators while at the same time being highly targeted by attackers. For years, organizations have tried to meet the regulatory and security demands of private data with some success as well as some failure. We explore the modern demands on private information from proactive data security, post-breach incident response, and industry regulatory requirements to the more recent consumer privacy requirements, all while highlighting public failure case studies and the questions business leaders should have been asking themselves to close inherent security gaps.

Keywords: Data compliance, threat detection, cloud transformation, breach, API, application programmable interface, PDPA, personal data protection Act, MAS, monetary authority of Singapore, cyber skills, encryption.

1. Personal Data Privacy, Industry Data Regulations, and Data Security — Three Sides of the Same Coin

Data security is driven by three primary factors: personal data privacy, industry data regulations, and security. Effectively, these are three sides of the same coin if coins had three sides. Using, storing, and sharing private data are necessary parts of doing business for modern organizations, while data remains highly governed by regulators yet highly targeted by attackers. For years, organizations have tried to meet the regulatory and security demands of private data with some successes and equal amounts of failures. In this chapter, we will explore security demands on private information from the perspectives of proactive data security, post-breach incident response, and industry regulatory requirements, as well as the more recent consumer privacy requirements. We will conclude with common questions business leaders should ask themselves to measure their current data security level in order to close inherent security gaps.

1.1. *Modernization and Pathways to Data Management*

As of 2024, we are still accelerating our modernization to the cloud or multi-cloud despite years of effort. Traditionally, we stored our systems and ran our businesses on premises. Today, the use of multiple cloud service providers is common for most organizations, yet they retain some infrastructure on premise in a hybrid simultaineous use of cloud and on premise. We, of course, have applications that, traditionally, were on premises but now have been modernized to include APIs, microservices, and cloud functions. And now the same thing is true of data management: Now data stores have been modernized into data lakes, data warehouses, file servers, online file storage, and anywhere in between, offering us on-premise, cloud, and fully managed options for storing data.

It is important to accept that there are necessary paths to data management that must both be allowed and secured, since businesses run on data, and the sharing and use of that data must be ensured. There are two fundamental paths to data management: accessed from outside of the organization and accessed from inside of the organization. Accessing data from inside the organization is often required for human users such as database administrators, data scientists, business users, and consultants, as well as non-human users like automation, applications, and even artificial intelligence.

External access to data is most commonly provided for web applications, APIs, and microservices, many of which are ungoverned by internal IT (Information Technology) and security teams due to the rapid business-driven modernizations. In the security industry, we recognize two groups of applications and APIs: those that we know about and those that we do not know about. Honest professionals acknowledge that both groups exist in almost every organization. We should therefore not be surprised that many organizations have no accurate map or list of every application and API that accesses their data; it is even less common that organizations have such a map included with the type of data each application or API interacts with. Data security requires that practitioners have at least some understanding of the conditions that exist for data assets needing protection, as well as how those conditions can impact protective data controls.

The overwhelming majority of transactions on organizational databases originate from applications and APIs. Organizations tend to trust these sources primarily because they are not human. A common control to build trust within an organization is identity access control, which should only be one aspect of securing data. Yet, for applications and APIs, it is often the only control, effectively positioning them as trusted "users" of a data store, when in fact little is known at the data layer about these "users" and the monitoring of their behavior is often inadequate.

Additionally, there is an entirely separate, though related, industry of web application security that recognizes the risk of applications and APIs and the fact that they are usually highly targeted and highly vulnerable.

1.2. *Stakeholders and Responsibility Ownership*

Data protection is about safeguarding data, regardless of who is accessing the data, whether it be applications, APIs, humans, or anyone else who has access to that critical asset. As there are multiple stakeholders within the organization, let us examine who among them holds responsibility for data.

Security and IT professionals are routinely tasked with implementing and managing the controls and tools associated with any kind of security, including data security. However, they often lack specific data security expertise or experience, leading them to apply more generic traditional access as well as end-point and perimeter controls in lieu of data security-focused solutions or processes.

As organizations have modernized, cloud architects have come into the picture, tasked with answering the following questions: What has been done to secure data as it is transformed and moved to the cloud? How do the controls and settings differ from on-premise data stores? How does data sovereignty apply, especially when data could reside physically outside of geo-political boundaries and outside of the purview of local regulations?

Executives and compliance officers who are tasked with ensuring various reporting and regulatory requirements are often curious about the best practices used in other organizations to secure data. They would want to know how their internal data security program and risk measurements compare to those of peer organizations and what their maturity plans are for risk and cost reduction.

Lastly, there is the general data user who like almost everyone, creates, edits, and deletes data as a part of their day to day job contributing to the explosion of organizational data in files and databases, often with little thought to how risky that data might be to the organization.

This brings us to the question of responsibility. Who is actually responsible for data security? Is it the Chief Information Officer (CIO), the Chief Information Security Officer (CISO), Data Privacy Officer (DPO), or the business unit? Or is it everyone? Is it the legal, risk, or compliance group that is responsible, or is it no one? Whose job is it to protect the data?

In an organization, it is critical to understand where this responsibility lands. It appears that the group with this responsibility has changed over time. If we rewind to the year 2000, responsibility belonged to the database administrator who was the designated manager of databases and naturally became the primary implementer of data security. These administrators knew where the data was, had control of the data store asset itself, and therefore were really the only people who had any knowledge of what should or should not be happening in their datasets.

An ever-escalating volume of attacks, exposures, and ultimately breaches throughout the 2000s and the early 2010s emphasized the fact that what we were doing was not working: A responsibility shift was imminent. We began to place the accountability for data security squarely on the team already responsible for the rest of corporate security, namely, the Chief Information Security Officer's team. There were some impediments to this, mostly in the forms of limited budget, small staff, and a skills gap that exists even today. Shifting the responsibility to the CISO's team enabled the identification of a technical owner with at least some traditional security expertise, if not specific to data security. The loss of data and volume of breaches nevertheless continued over the years.

While industry-specific data regulations were nothing new in the mid-2010s, it was the unification and simplification of European personal data privacy regulations and the potentially massive fines that the General Data Protection Regulation (GDPR) imposed in 2016 that finally mandated responsibility to an entirely new role focused on personally identifiable data — the Data Privacy Officer (DPO).

The result is that we have two responsible functions: the DPO, who is often involved in the legal or risk-related domains, and the CISO, who is responsible for security technology and its implementation. Now, rather than a single owner of data security, we have a divergence, where it can be difficult to determine who actually holds the responsibility for data security. Is it the DPO team with their requirements for reporting, processes, and protection? Is it the CISO's team and the people who implement technology who also have requirements for reporting and protection? The reality is that the answer changes from organization to organization as each organization bases its decision on its industry, regulations, operational regions, and organizational structure.

The final decision of which team is responsible is less important than the actual act of assigning responsibility to an owner and holding them accountable.

1.3. *Factors Influencing Data Security Today*

There is no question that data is the most critical asset many organizations have, particularly the most critical asset that when lost can never be returned. Once it's out, it's out. Threats on data are not only growing in frequency but also increasing in complexity. It has become more challenging to model indicative bad behaviors, yet these threats are easier than ever to execute. Modern threat actors utilize the service of hacking for hire, which has been enabled by the development of automated tools including those powered by artificial intelligence.

We know the impacts of a breach or exposure can include regulatory fines, brand damage, identity theft, loss of customers, and the often overlooked outcome of tighter regulations. As a result of the ever-growing volumes of breaches, complex threats, and organizational failures in data protection, industry and governments have stepped in to fill the gap with mandated global cybersecurity regulations. We already have more than 150 global cybersecurity regulations with more on the way.

Regulated or not, among the first questions asked after a data breach or exposure is the following: Why? Data loss happens for a reason and there are a series of regular failure points.

The following are some of the common reasons why data loss takes place:

- Organizations move data to unusual or unexpected places.
- Data stores are not monitored, leaving security blind.

- There is no owner for data security.
- We focus less on our legacy systems and more on modern systems.
- We are ignorant of security in our modern systems because we do not have the skills to understand the security around them.
- We lack general data security expertise throughout the CISO or DPO functions.
- We focus only on compliance and do not implement effective data security practices.

Yet another major challenge comes from the realization that data stores of all types have drastically changed over the years. Traditionally, as we mentioned earlier, a data store was just a relational database. Now, the data estate or landscape includes big data systems in the varying forms of data lakes, data warehouses, and data marts. The exponential increase in the volume of files in on-premise file servers, as well as those in the cloud, poses unique challenges. Storing and using data residing in these locations compound the challenge of monitoring all access and building adequate security into data activity.

1.4. *Motivating Data Security Behavior*

Given everything we have read so far, it may seem obvious that the motivating factor for developing a data security program is preventing data breaches and exposures, but that is not often the case. Let us look closer at what drives organizations to develop data security programs.

Unfortunately, we do not simply say, "We implement data security, because it's obviously what we should do," even though it is what we should do. Evidence from major breaches shows that the motivation for organizations to implement data security programs is not what most of us would think. What drives organizations to provide security or monitoring for their data is primarily regulatory compliance, not the recognition that you need to protect data as a course of best practice.

When we ask organizations whether they should protect data, their response is unanimously, yes.

When we ask organizations to stack rank data security among their other cybersecurity priorities, data security is always a top-three priority, higher yet in highly regulated industries like financial services and healthcare. When we ask organizations if meeting regulatory compliance requirements is equal to or better than having data security controls based on industry-recognized frameworks, they again provide a unanimous answer, *but the answer is now no.*

When we interviewed security and risk teams looking for data security solutions and asked what capabilities they are looking to gain from security technologies, they cited one regulation or another that they needed to meet. Surprisingly the need for an effective program to protect data rarely comes up as a response. This scenario leads us to the following requirements:

- Discover all data stores and determine the location of regulated data based on the regulations driving them.
- Monitor "only" database administrator (privileged user) access to the regulated data, usually only for production systems.
- Detect, alert, and sometimes prevent threats on the regulated data. Not all organizations are interested in the prevention of unwanted data activity, many only want to report on it.
- Store access logs for 1–7 years.

The gains that organizations seek are not all bad; they simply restrict a data security program to small silos of data and data stores due to a strict focus on specific types of regulated data. Creating a data security program prioritized by regulatory compliance, and thereby applying controls only on regulated data, leaves all other data and data stores without security or monitoring. Consider whether security teams apply this same targeted or silo practice to any other pillars of security within their responsibility.

Are there network firewalls only on networks with regulated data or systems and nowhere else?

Is anti-virus or anti-malware applied only to systems with regulated data on them and nowhere else?

Do we apply single sign-on and multi-factor authorization only to regulated systems and nowhere else?

Across the board, the answer should be no. Best-practice cybersecurity is routinely applied to all other security pillars, for all networks, end points, and authorizations, except the pillar of the data security. Regarding data security, while regulatory compliance has provided general directions for organizations to protect specific data, it has simultaneously created a false sense of security as organizations prioritize passing regulatory audits over mapping data security to industry-standard security frameworks like the National Institute of Standards and Technology (NIST) or the SANS Institute.

1.5. *Dispelling the Misnomer "Data Security is Hard"*

When we think fundamentally about data security and compliance, there are only a few simple questions that must be answered to show that organizations have a best-practice data security program:

- *Who* accessed the data?
- *What* data did they access?
- *When* did they access the data?
- From *where* did they access the data?
- *How* did they access the data?
- *Should* they access the data at all?

Organizations that can answer these questions rapidly, reliably, completely, and accurately have laid the groundwork for an effective data security program.

Now that we understand the types of questions organizations should be able to answer about their data, let us understand how we should use the collected data activity beyond compliance reporting.

The answers to the questions who, what, when, where, how, and should are critical for understanding threat detection behavior. At its core, data security is the ability to identify unusual behavior in data activity and to confidently apply security controls. Yet, it is critical to collect data activity information with ample volume, variety, and veracity in order to analyze it, oftentimes through machine learning or AI (Artificial Intelligence). In a traditional cyber-security sense, it is the ability to take vast volumes of data activity information and distill from that actionable incidents.

Traditionally, data security incidents provide very little context, leaving the workload of incident response and research to security teams who, as we previously noted, often lack database and file activity security skill sets. Therefore, effective data security programs and supporting technologies must automate the translation of Structured Query Language (SQL) into detailed, contextual incidents for Security Operations Center (SOC) personnel to rapidly prioritize and respond without the need for excessive cross-functional collaboration.

1.6. *How Mature Data Security Programs Define their Capabilities*

Throughout this chapter, we learned about key factors related to data security, including responsibility and ownership, the paths to data management, and drivers influencing and motivating organizational action. Organizations that successfully implement data security practices for security, and not simply compliance, have several common requirements.

There are six primary requirements for protecting data estates at a high level:

- Support for on-premise and multi-cloud data assets.
- Data activity collection and analysis at scale to support all data in any organization.
- Compliance and incident response reporting.

- Threat detection from any source including humans, applications, and APIs.
- Reduction of the need for specialized cybersecurity skills.
- Integration with existing ecosystem cybersecurity technologies.

If we map the above-mentioned high-level requirements to specific security industry technologies, then we find the following product types:

- Database Activity Monitoring,
- File Activity Monitoring,
- Web Application and API Security,
- Identity Access Management,
- Anomaly Detection and Prevention,
- Data Discovery and Classification,
- Data Encryption, Tokenization, and Masking,
- Cloud-Native Data Security.

As we mentioned previously, these technologies must include coverage for all locations of organizational data, whether on premises or in multi-cloud, as well as every type of data, structured, semi-structured (Big Data), and unstructured. Traditionally, and to a lesser degree still today, these technologies have been offered as individual vendor solutions. The data security industry, however, matures like everything else and has more recently seen a transition toward unified multi-product, single-vendor data security platforms, inclusive of many or all layers of the above-mentioned product stack, in lieu of distinct multi-vendor point solutions.

The intent behind both data security and regulatory compliance is simple: to protect data. They diverge primarily around their scope and breadth, but they still expect the same outcomes for the data they target. Let us review the previously discussed acknowledgments made by security professionals that data is important, its protection is a priority, and compliance is not the same as data security. In this, we would do well to remember that when tasked with the responsibility of protecting data, we will be measured by *both* our strategies to reduce the risk of a breach and our strategies to reduce the risk of non-compliance. When we consider the alternative strategy of *choosing* compliance *over* security, we then accept levels of risk that rapidly become unacceptable and expensive during post-breach activities.

1.7. *Regulatory and Security Evaluation Questions*

Lastly, we will review two sets of questions: those that organizations can expect auditors to ask during an audit and those that organizations should ask themselves to get an idea about the current data security efficacy.

While regulations have much in common, their requirements often need some interpretation, which leads to varying organizational experiences with auditors. The regulatory requirement questions in the following are a sample of those commonly posed to financial services, insurance, and healthcare, which are also the industries most regulated and most highly targeted by bad actors.

1.7.1. *Questions organizations should commonly expect from regulatory auditors*

- Provide a record of all user login failures.
- Provide a record of material changes made to regulated data.
- Provide a report of all new users added.
- Provide a map and proof of all data stores having regulated data.
- Provide proof that regulated data does not exist in non-production systems and if it does exist, show that it has been redacted, masked, or tokenized.
- Provide proof that regulated data does not exist in non-production systems and if it does exist, show that it has been redacted, masked, or tokenized.
- Demonstrate monitoring of all accesses to regulated data.
- Demonstrate detection of unusual behavior.

- Report each user's access role and the last time the user account was used.
- Report on the hygiene of orphan and unused data users.
- Show disabled access for orphan and unused users over one year.
- Demonstrate long-term data access log retention from 1 to 7 years.

As we established previously, regulation, unfortunately, drives most data security programs today, but there are core capabilities organizations must have in order to meet the regulatory demands and also rise to the higher purpose of effectively securing data. Organizations that can quickly and accurately answer these questions about their own environment are leading the industry in data security maturity.

1.7.2. *Questions organizations should ask themselves to evaluate their own data security maturity*

- Can we report on *every* user accessing *all* data on *all* data stores?
  - o Users include humans, applications, APIs, and others.
- Are there means to rapidly identify *what* data a user accessed and how many records were accessed?
  - o For *any* given data store can we answer *any* question regarding activity and access for incident response or regulation?
  - o Are there acceptable plans and understanding of risk in place if we cannot answer this?
- Can we determine unusual data activity quickly enough to prevent loss of data?
  - o Including analysis of humans and application access.
- Can we identify users who have authorized access to data, but who have in fact not used that access and should potentially have their access removed until it is needed?
  - o This includes dormant users defined as unused access past a period of time.

- Have we defined a responsible person, team, or function for data security and have they taken ownership of the program and the outcomes?
- Can we map every location of regulated as well as other important unregulated data throughout the organization?
  - o Can we prove that this data does not reside in unexpected locations?

1.8. *Concluding Thoughts*

In this chapter, we have detailed how data security today is driven by three primary factors: personal data privacy, industry data regulations, and security. And while we know these factors require specific technology and expertise for best-practice security, organizations have routinely opted for lesser controls commonly solving for regulatory compliance rather than their stated goal of data security and protection. Before we can be assured that our data security program is complete, it is imperative to revisit our organizational data security goals and note how well our implemented people, processes, and controls work together toward those objectives. We have seen that it is too easy to fall into complacency where holistic data security is reduced to targeted regulated data security because of a passed regulatory audit. This provides a false assurance that the targeted regulated data program is effective, when in fact it may not be for the larger organizational footprint. Successful organizations recognize the need to protect data for the sake of security in addition to the need for targeted controls on regulated data. Unfortunately, the primary catalyst for maturing organizational data security is the personal experience of a data breach where security teams are immediately tasked with re-evaluating their programs and strategies. The hope is that those of us tasked with the responsibility of data security and regulatory compliance will remain vigilant in our efforts to achieve the primary goal of protecting data because it is the right thing to do, not just because someone told us to, as they would for compliance.

Chapter 6

Privacy-First Design — The Significant Role of Privacy-Enhancing Technologies

Sowmya Ganapathi Krishnan

Thoughtworks APAC, Chicago, USA
skrishnan@thoughtworks.com

Abstract

In today's data-driven world, organizations must treat personal data with the utmost respect. Ensuring privacy is critical for organizations when it comes to building digital trust with customers. There is a major misconception that it is difficult to protect data privacy while gaining insights from organizational data. Privacy-Enhancing Technologies (PETs) help to correct this misconception. Personal data can be protected while still being used for specific purposes by organizations using Privacy-Enhancing Technologies (PETs). By enabling businesses to incorporate privacy into their services, products, and business processes right from the beginning, PETs enable a data privacy-first design. PETs have been emphasized as one of the key technological enablers in SGTech's study on the state of digital trust. In this chapter, we look at why privacy-first design is important, how PETs offer a novel method for safeguarding data privacy, the privacy vs utility trade-off, and finally who is responsible for data privacy in our organizations.

Keywords: Privacy, privacy-enhancing technologies, homomorphic encryption, secure multi-party computation, differential privacy, federated learning.

The last two decades have seen an explosion of data generation, thanks to the proliferation of social media, easier access to the internet, and very affordable and scalable storage and computing resources. 90% of the data accumulated globally were generated in the last 2 years, and this is poised to double every two years! Growth in social media, communication technologies, digital image creation applications, and IoT is contributing to this explosion. Needless to say, data leaders and practitioners also find themselves in an exciting and equally challenging time.

It is inevitable that a significant percentage of the data generated is personally identifiable. We log on to Facebook, upload a photo, and tag a friend. We register our WhatsApp contact on the cloud with our phone numbers or visit an e-commerce site and enter our address for delivery. Every touchpoint on the internet is capturing one or another facet of our identity. As data practitioners, it is important to ensure that the processes, policies, and technologies that we develop and deploy inspire digital trust by protecting individual privacy preferences. In this chapter, we will discuss how organizations can strike a balance between protecting data privacy and gaining insights from data.

1. Data Privacy and Digital Trust

The SGTech Digital Trust Landscape study defines digital trust as "the confidence digital participants have to interact safely, securely, and in a transparent, accountable, and frictionless manner." When one interacts with a website, the right to decline sharing non-essential personal information and the confidence that the provided information will not be used for any unintended purposes encourage one to keep visiting the site. This ensures trust building with the enterprise.

Digital Trust

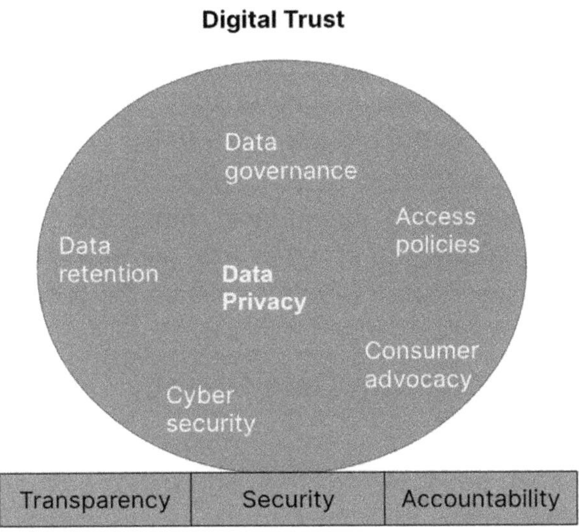

Building this trust is what enables businesses to grow. Contrary to what we usually hear, ensuring data privacy is good for business. Government bodies need to ensure adherence to policies, protecting citizens' rights, enabling businesses to be accountable, and facilitating universal access to data for policymaking. The following consumer research study from 2022 illustrates that consumers value data privacy from businesses, and brands need to align with consumer perspectives on privacy to drive trust and business value.

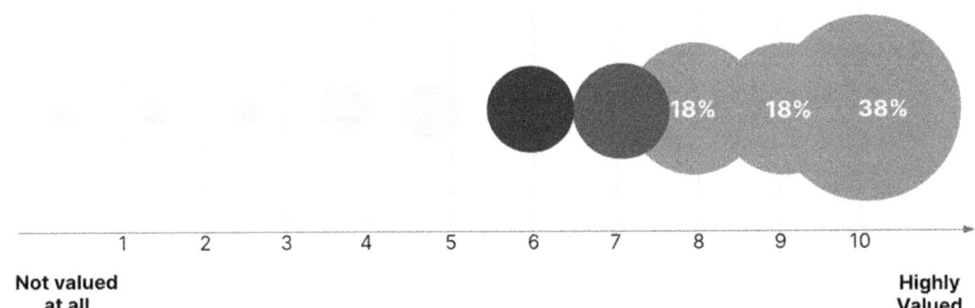

Source: MAGNA, Ketch, UM — US Consumer Research Study 2022.
Respondents were asked, "How much do you value data privacy?" [1–10 scale].

Beyond losing user confidence, the costs and risks of neglecting data privacy are very high. Every year, the number of data breaches is growing significantly, despite efforts. Such data breaches erode the trust that customers have in a business and drive away existing and future customers. The average cost of a data breach was $4.35 million (US) in 2022, reaching $5M in 2023. Engineering teams on the ground pay interest on privacy debt and take on much more effort to patch gaps in existing live production systems with personally identifiable information. This, consequently, leaves patched-up systems that are prone to a breach at any time, like a live electric wire left bare on the ground.

2. Why Has Protecting Data Privacy Been Difficult?

Regulations such as HIPAA, GDPR, and PDPA have enforced the need for organizations to adhere to the requirements to preserve individual privacy. With every new regulation, organizations enter a catch-up game, revisiting their data privacy implementation procedures and processes. As a result, every data breach results in a patch and ends with a secret hope that it does not happen anytime in the near future.

In 1995, Ann Cavoukian developed an approach to systems engineering called "privacy by design." Privacy by design calls for privacy to be taken into account throughout the entire engineering process. Some of the foundational principles stated in the approach include the following:

- Respect for an individual's privacy should be the top priority, to be addressed proactively rather than reactively.
- Privacy should be embedded into all aspects of the product creation life cycle to reduce business risk and impact of data breaches.
- Privacy is not a zero-sum game: One can create a win-win situation yet address user privacy preferences at the core.

These are very sensible principles, but why do we see limited implementation of these on the ground? Most of the enterprises I have spoken with feel that there is no way to gain insights from the data if they focused on preserving data privacy. Data privacy becomes a game of "passing the parcel" in many places; IT ends up implementing it even though it is not close to the data generated by the various business domains. There is a lack of awareness of the ecosystem that could enable one to preserve data privacy and yet utilize the data for further analytics. The following points broadly summarize the reasons why privacy by design has been so difficult at many enterprises:

1. Lack of awareness of privacy-enhancing technologies
2. Lack of understanding of the privacy vs utility trade-off.
3. Lack of sufficient accountability to drive privacy by design or privacy-first design.

In the forthcoming sections, we aim to address these challenges one by one. Latch on to your seatbelts!

2.1. *A Tour of Privacy-Enhancing Technologies (PETs)*

Privacy by design originated from Privacy-Enhancing Technologies (PETs) in a joint 1995 report by Ann Cavoukian and John Borking. PETs are techniques that aim to preserve data privacy by enabling computations on data without revealing any sensitive information about the underlying entities. PETs have become mainstream now given the major emphasis coming from the United Nations, the US Whitehouse, the European and Singapore media, and reports and guidelines released by regulatory bodies and regulatory sandboxes around the use of PETs.

How is it possible to not reveal any sensitive information while we perform computations? Let us see how PETs achieve this. We are going to explore 4 common use cases in order to understand how PETs can enable the preservation of data privacy and yet provide the necessary insights.

3. Understanding Customer Behavior without Compromising on Privacy

Every organization that sells goods to consumers has pondered the following questions: "What can I offer that consumers want?" "Which demographic should I target?" "How can I cross-sell my products to the customers who may be interested in buying?" Customer behavior analysis is at the heart of top-line growth for enterprises.

Yet, it has been a challenge to look at customer data and infer insights as enterprises struggle to balance privacy and utility. What if we can encrypt the customer's personal information and yet be able to infer the behavioral patterns? That would be fantastic, wouldn't it? Our first PET star candidate: homomorphic encryption.

Homomorphic encryption refers to a class of encryption methods that allow computations to be performed directly on encrypted data. The result would be decryptable only by a specific party that has access to the secret key, typically the owner of the input data. The term "homo morphic" translates to similar shape, indicating that the shape of the encrypted data mimics that of the raw data.

Let's say Company X has a set of customer-consented data elements and wants to use a third-party service provider to perform customer research. The data owner from company X generates a homomorphic public–private key pair, encrypts the customer-consented data elements with the private key, and sends across the encrypted data and the public key to the third-party vendor.

The third-party service provider uses the homomorphic data processing algorithm enabling it to perform computations on the encrypted customer data and share the encrypted insights with the data owner. The data owner then decrypts the insights with the private key. Still hovering at a very high level of how homomorphic

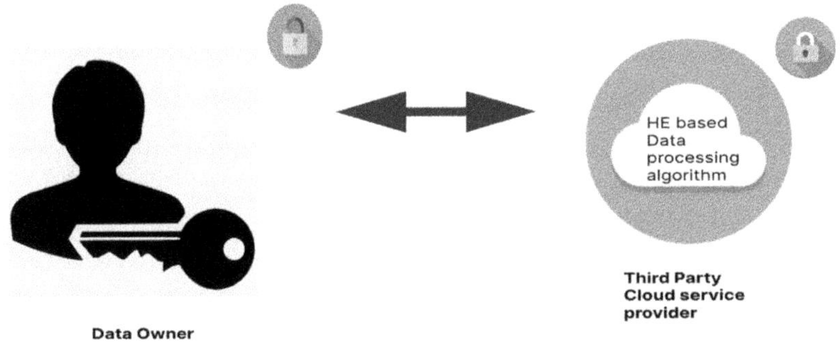

encryption works, it gives us the assurance that this technique can help firms have the same processing possibilities that they have on raw data, with an encrypted set. Imagine the use cases possible if this technique is made widely available!

The technique is already in use in several fields including health analytics and customer behavior analysis. There has been a lot of open-source effort in this space. Some prominent libraries include IBM HeLib, Palisade, OpenFHE, TFHE, HEAAN, and Microsoft SEAL. There have been several white papers on HME and the security of HME in particular. The HME standard can be found here[1] in detail for further reading.

4. Linking Anonymized Medical Records across Agencies to Promote Healthy Lifestyle

A few years ago, my team was working on an effort to link the medical records of citizens to enable smart nudges that would encourage healthy lifestyles. The challenge was ensuring the identity of the citizens was preserved as we were dealing with sensitive medical and personal information. We started to explore ways to overcome this challenge and came across this powerful PET that

---

[1] https://homomorphicencryption.org/wp-content/uploads/2018/11/HomomorphicEncryption Standardv1.1.pdf.

is at the core of secure data sharing called Secure Multi-Party Computation.

Secure multi-party computation is a subfield of cryptography with the goal of creating methods for parties to jointly compute a function over their inputs while keeping those inputs confidential. In a utopia, we can trust everyone. In reality, we do not have the luxury of having a Trusted Third Party who can take care of performing processing on private data, but practically it makes sense to represent this TTP algorithmically instead.

What does SMPC do differently? SMPC deals with the problem of jointly computing an agreed-upon function (data processing) among a set of possibly semi-trusting parties (parties who follow the protocol but are interested in others' data) while preventing any participant from learning anything about the inputs provided by other parties, and while guaranteeing (to the extent possible) that the correct output is achieved.

Let me walk you through an example:

A customer submits a hospitalization claim to an insurance company. The insurance company requests the hospital to help in the calculation of the payable items less deductibles and co-insurance. Since the customer is using a bank-issued credit card, the reimbursed amount needs to be transferred to the credit card. This transaction needs to be performed by the hospital, insurance company, and the bank without revealing the sensitive details of the customer to one another. All the parties implement an SMPC

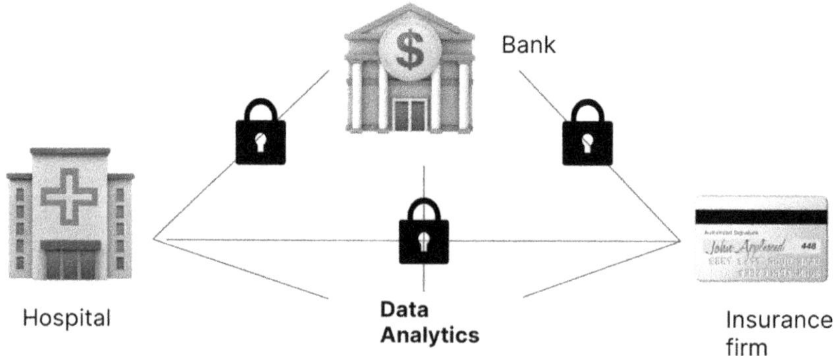

protocol, using a set of instructions and intercommunications that implement a distributed computer program.

As part of this program, their respective data records are divided into two or more shares and these shares are homomorphically encrypted (yes, the method explained earlier). The encrypted versions of the shares are distributed to the hospital, bank, and the insurance company. The homomorphic properties of addition and multiplication allow for those parties to compute on the shares they received to attain shared results, which when combined produce the correct output of the data processing.

At any point during this processing, no one can decrypt their share as it is a split driven by the protocol and only the owner of the dataset who holds the private key can decrypt it back.

The ability to participate in a transaction securely makes SMPC protocols extremely significant for common user base identification between companies, secure data analysis and sharing, crypto wallets, e-auctions, e-voting, and several others. There are multiple products and solutions based on SMPC that make it easier for one to onboard and start using this protocol, without significant effort.

5. Sharing Insights Broadly without Revealing Sensitive Data

In the 2020 census, the US Census Bureau decided that it had to adhere to the longstanding requirement to ensure that the data from individuals and individual households remain confidential. It planned to use an approach called "differential privacy" to achieve this.

The idea behind differential privacy is that for analytical use cases, we rely not on the individual data points but rather on the aggregates.

Differential Privacy is the effect of making an arbitrary single substitution in the database small enough that the query result cannot be used to infer much about any single individual and therefore provides privacy. How did the US Census Bureau utilize differential privacy at a high level?

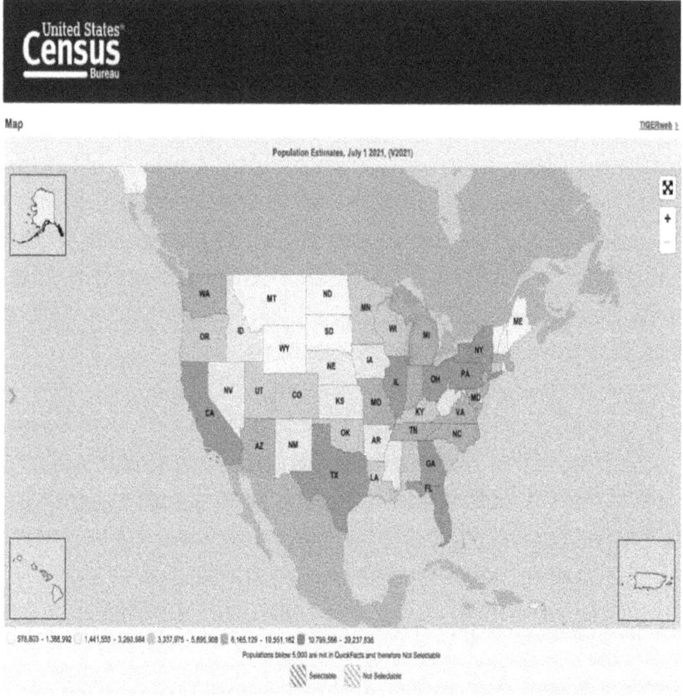

One approach is by adding calibrated noise to the census numbers without losing the statistical integrity. Differential privacy helps to achieve the trade-off that enables us to add noise to the individual data points while maintaining the broader aggregate accuracy. Let's say you are holding a painting in your hand. At every pixel, you zoom in and add a few small dots. When zoomed in, these dots are clearly visible. But, when we zoom out, the painting still seems unaltered. That is what differential privacy does to datasets. By carefully calibrating noise to the individual data points, the US Census Bureau was able to broadly make the statistics available for wider use, without worry about individual re-identification risk.

Differential privacy has been widely used by many companies such as Apple and Uber for a long while now. It holds a lot of potential in enabling wider release of datasets without compromising on privacy. That means secure sharing of public data with citizens, secure analysis of customer behavior, privacy-enhancing recommender systems, and more.

5.1. *How can Data be Crowdsourced without Sharing? Can we Crowdsource without Sharing Data?*

Let us visit one last PET that has proved to be the golden key to building privacy-preserving AI. Every day, there is a new threat emerging in the industry, especially in the financial sector. Every financial institution is in the process of building a fraud detection model to evaluate every transaction, to protect the reputation of the institution, and to adhere to the regulatory guidelines. But detecting fraud is not a single-enterprise game. It is important to work together to build a robust model to tackle this with all the patterns the banking and financial industry has seen. How can we achieve this when one institution cannot share sensitive records with another?

Federated learning helps achieve these goals. As the name suggests, federated learning allows many parties to train a model together without aggregating the data in a centralized location. Instead of sending data, the parties train locally and send small vectorized updates to an aggregator.

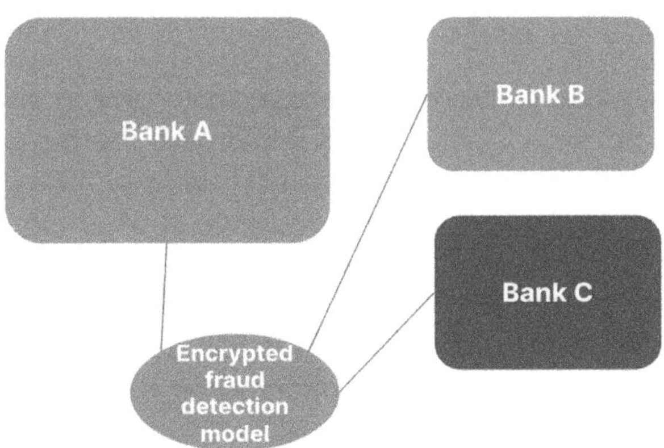

A generic baseline fraud detection model is stored at the central server. The copies of this model are shared with participating banking institutions, who then train the models based on the local transaction data that they handle. Over time, the models in the respective banks become contextualized for the nature of the institution — the segments they target, the customer demographics, and others.

In the next stage, the updates (model parameters) from the locally trained models from the banking institutions are shared with the main model located at the central server using secure aggregation techniques. This model combines and averages different inputs to generate new learnings. Since the data are collected from diverse sources, there is greater scope for the model to become generalizable.

Once the central model has been retrained on new parameters at the aggregator, it is shared with the banks for the next iteration. With every cycle, the models gather a varied amount of information and improve further without creating privacy breaches. The only way we can build intelligence is to crowdsource our capabilities together, and federated learning helps institutions build stronger algorithms together.

Health and FinTech are domains that could greatly benefit from federated learning. Any domain that demands building a privacy-preserving machine learning model across multiple parties needs a federated learning approach.

6. Summary of PETs

Privacy-Enhancing Technologies are a must-have in our toolbox to enable data privacy. It helps us to implement the privacy vs utility trade-off needed for any analytical use case in today's world. In the following, we present a quick revision of what we read in this chapter.

Homomorphic encryption — great for confidential computing where the user can encrypt and decrypt the data before and after processing the data.

Secure multi-party computation — data sharing should one day be all encrypted and/or anonymized.

Differential privacy — Best fit for sensitive data minimization in basic use cases.

Federated learning — One of the best privacy-preserving machine learning technologies available.

Next, we will discuss privacy vs utility trade-offs. Do not unlatch your seat belts yet, the privacy ride continues!

7. Privacy vs. Utility Trade-Off

More often than not, data practitioners think that privacy and utility are exclusive in nature. Anonymized data fields mean they are no longer relevant. In the previous section, that is the exact argument that we are negating by means of privacy-enhancing technologies. With the usage of anonymization techniques such as redaction, hashing, or privacy-enhancing technologies, it is important to understand the privacy vs utility trade-off.

In the illustration above, we see two personas on either side of the acceptable trade-off.

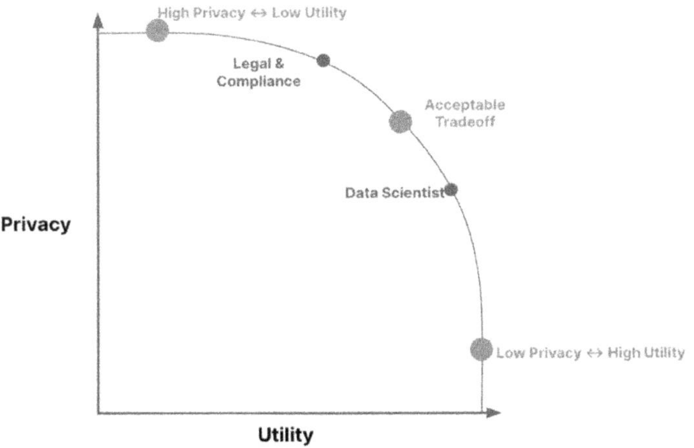

1. **Legal and compliance team** — Entrusted with the need to define data protection policies, monitor internal compliance, and mitigate any risks for the firm around personal data usage. This team is always geared to enforce the highest data privacy mechanisms, enabling the firm to adhere to the regulatory guidelines.
2. **Data scientists** — On the other side of the spectrum are our data analysts and scientists who have been tasked to explore and analyze the data and derive insights from the same to aid in company growth. Although they want to ensure data privacy, they always want to get their hands on as much customer-consented data as possible to aid in their analytics.

7.1. *What is an Acceptable Trade-Off?*

An "acceptable" trade-off has to consider all sides: the legal and risk appetite of the company, the use case one is tasked with solving, and most importantly the users that feature in the data. Whatever the mandates of the company, the trade-off is primarily decided by what types of consents have been provided by the users for data utilization and the granularity levels of data use approved by users. As a data practitioner, it is important that we enable privacy by design by enforcing the collection of granular consents in the application flow and ensuring these consents are directed toward the privacy vs utility trade-off in the analytics life cycle.

One could argue that enforcing consent management might not be the responsibility of a data practitioner, who is usually involved only when the data flow from operational to analytical planes. Who should be responsible for privacy by design then? An important question to address. In the next and last section of this chapter, we will discuss the most important part of enforcing data privacy — "accountability."

8. Driving Accountability for Data Privacy in Your Organization

The life of a data strategist can be summed up as "40% driving accountability, 30% enforcing process, 30% automation through

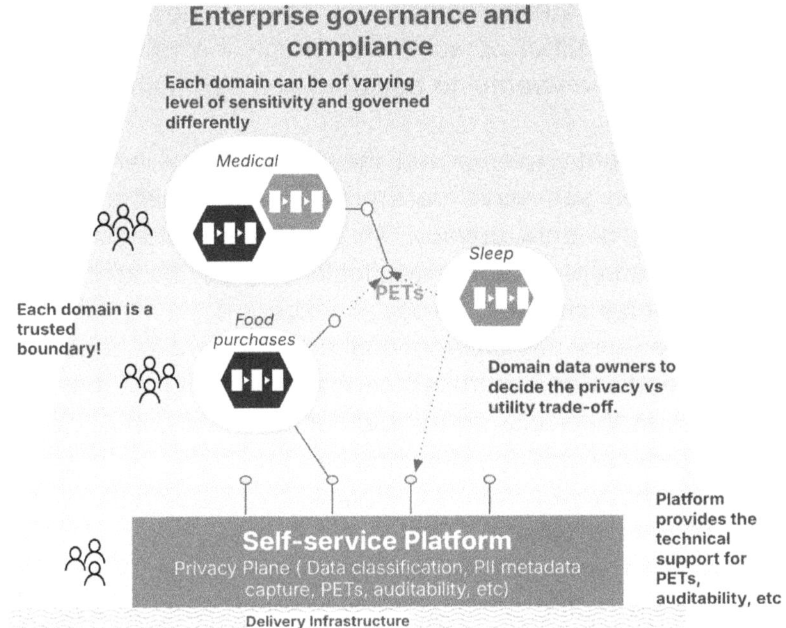

technology." Driving accountability for the various stewardship initiatives is the most arduous and time-consuming task in data governance. Who is responsible for experimenting on PETs, understanding their use cases, weighing the privacy vs utility trade-off, and ultimately owning the responsibility for creating privacy-first design?

Federated computational governance enables one to think about the responsibility not as one person's task, but rather as distributed among the various business domains and the central council at the enterprise level.

A domain here is defined by the boundary within which teams and systems revolve around an agreed-upon business objective. From the illustration above, you can see domains that are frequently seen when we are tracking health metrics. Medical information, sleep data, and food purchases are exemplary domains in health promotion. The data owners of these respective domains understand the nature of the data, the users, the sensitivity of the domain, and consequently the privacy needs. These domain data owners are the rightful personnel to weigh the privacy vs utility trade-off and do the needful to transform their domains into trusted boundaries.

We should centrally empower these domain owners by providing a centralized self-serve data platform that enables the easy implementation of data privacy. This includes data classification tools, metadata capture and classification, anonymization tool kits, and privacy-enhancing technology tool kits.

Enterprise-level compliance and enforcement of legal needs might still need to be controlled centrally, keeping all the domain data owners in the loop, and implemented on a centralized platform. This ensures that the domains can focus only on implementing their specific privacy needs without worrying about those cutting across multiple domains.

In a nutshell, privacy is everyone's responsibility! Whether you are a data owner, data scientist, software engineer, or legal practitioner, everyone is dealing with user data and needs to bring to life privacy-first design principles in their context.

In summary:

- Create products with privacy built-in right from the beginning of the software development life cycle.
- Increase awareness of PETs in your organization to implement a privacy-first design.
- Empower your teams to implement the privacy vs utility trade-off in their respective domains.

Privacy is not an option but a prerequisite for anyone dealing with the usage and exchange of data. As data professionals, the upcoming years will prove to be a testing time for data privacy given the exponential breakthrough of Gen AI. But, with the right foundational principles in hand, we will be able to handle data privacy well, ensuring digital trust at the core of what we do.

Chapter 7

Data Strategy and AI Value Creation: Dataspaces — Opportunities with ESG

Marcus Hartmann,[*] **Felix Baumann**[†] **and Elisa Lederer**[‡]

PwC Germany, Berlin, Germany
[*]marcus.hartmann@pwc.com
[†]felix.baumann@pwc.com
[‡]elisa.lederer@pwc.com

Abstract

This chapter provides an overview of the current developments in the European Union (EU) that require more sustainable, digital, and environmental, social, and corporate governance (ESG) conformance of business activities as well as the opportunities that come with it. With an increasingly digitized economy and sustainability reporting obligations in place, data sharing will gain in importance and become a central enabler toward a green and data-driven EU single market. Therefore, this chapter aims to cover the legislative initiatives pushing for the use of dataspaces. It also provides an overview of the current dataspace landscape and the stakeholders who actively shape the usability, understanding, and technical frameworks to bring dataspaces to life. Additionally, it explores the risks and opportunities associated with the commercial use of dataspaces for ESG reporting in different industries and showcases examples of both functioning dataspaces that came to life and those that remained an idea. Ultimately, this chapter carves out ESG-related options and considerations for value creation for Chief Data Officers (CDOs) working in European companies or within companies operating in the EU single market.

Keywords: Data sharing, regulation, sustainability data, digital economy, EU data, ESG, reporting, business innovation, CDO/ Chief Data Officer.

1. Introduction

Europe's business environment is increasingly driven by sustainability desires and the need to become data-driven. With the start of Ursula von der Leyen's presidency of the European Commission in 2020, the EU took on an ambitious course toward climate neutrality by 2050 with the "European Green Deal" (European Commission, 2019a) while also declaring "Europe's Digital Decade" (European Commission, 2019b). This was in response to the growing demand for sustainable business practices and the ever-increasing amount of industrial data and digitalization demands necessitated by changes in demographics within the European economy.

The developments are also in line with market trends and changing consumer preferences in the EU. Businesses are expanding their activity in online markets, slowly surpassing traditional analogue models and adapting to changing consumer preferences. In the EU, the turnover of online businesses has grown by over 70% since 2017, reaching an estimated €712.5 billion this year (Beyrouthy, 2023). In addition, the values and priorities of young Europeans differ in comparison to other generations. Rather than business growth, European 16–26-year-olds prioritize raising awareness about sustainability and fighting climate change (YouGov, 2022). The majority hence calls for government intervention in climate protection through taxation and regulatory measures, putting pressure on political decision-makers to include these aspects in future legislation.

In this light, strategic data usage and the role of a Chief Data Officer (CDO) are gaining more importance. CDOs hold the only company position that interfaces with the data-related responsibilities arising from legislative requirements and business innovation ambitions. The changes envisioned by European lawmakers will disrupt the way companies run their day-to-day business and necessitate major changes. CDOs are in a position to help with both getting the right data to meet the regulatory and reporting requirements and driving business innovation with data so as to stay competitive. With increasing technical requirements and the approaching ESG reporting obligations, CDOs hold a central and interfacing role to make a difference in the way companies deal with the new and mandatory collection of data. This chapter discusses how the different streams in the European economy can be consolidated and used as an opportunity to leverage technical infrastructures such as dataspaces and ESG reporting.

2. Dataspaces as a Solution for European Ambitions

Legislative measures and initiatives were developed in response to the shift in societal and political priorities in the EU to provide technical frameworks and prepare the economy for upcoming challenges (Curry *et al.*, 2022, p. 2). Furthermore, technological developments and the ever-increasing amount of data generated have influenced those legislative measures. The following section will discuss these measures in terms of legislation, governance, and public disclosure.

2.1. *Legislative Landscape*

Appropriate legislation has been put in place by the EU lawmakers to meet the two long-term goals of the European economy: the green transition and digitalization. The latter aims to make better use of data and drive digital transformation with concrete goals: The European Commission plans to have 75% of businesses utilize cloud, artificial intelligence (AI), and big data technologies, while also ensuring that 90% of small and medium-sized enterprises (SMEs) achieve a minimum level of digital intensity by 2030 (European Commission, 2022c, p. 3).

As an answer to the growing relevance of data, EU bodies released the European Data Strategy (European Commission, 2020) that aims to make data more accessible in the EU. It also aims to provide high-quality data to start-ups, SMEs, the public sector, and enterprises in general to facilitate innovation and business growth. The expected increase in data usage in the European Union will be regulated by several acts under the EU Data Strategy, with the EU Data Act and the EU Data Governance Act being the most recent ones. These acts aim to make data sharing in the European Union more transparent and safe while providing clear and fair rules for the access and use of data.

Additionally, the EU is working on making sustainability an integral part of its financial policy in order to support the European Green Deal. To do so, a stringent EU taxonomy was implemented, with requirements for supply chain contracts and benchmarks on meeting environmental, social, and corporate governance (ESG) as well as corporate social responsibility (CSR) criteria for all business activities in the EU. The two terms are often used interchangeably to describe sustainability ambitions. They overlap in terms of demonstrating companies' commitment to sustainable business practices (Lutkevich, 2023). But despite having overlaps, they differ in their scope, which the EU has recently concretized and tightened.

One way to describe the main difference is as follows: While CSR can be seen as the overall idea on sustainable business practice at the company level, ESG takes a detail-oriented quantitative perspective. ESG is crucial for future businesses within the EU as the sustainability progress of firms will be verified through reporting from 2025 onward through the Corporate Sustainability Reporting Directive (CSRD) that came into effect in January 2023. The new

ESG reporting standards presented in the CSRD will apply to some 50,000 firms and will have a far-reaching impact. For example, based on ESG data, public funding bodies will make decisions on granting loans to companies for large-scale investments and business activities within the EU.

In addition, an EU supply chain law will soon come into force, which will implement certain due diligence obligations for companies in order to prevent their business activities from having negative impacts on human rights and the environment along their chains of activity within and outside Europe (Federal Ministry of Labour and Social Affairs, 2023).

With these developments in mind, the need for more data exchange becomes evident. Dataspaces generate the opportunity to ensure safe, efficient, and reliable data sharing in a trusted and regulated technical framework and environment. The overview in Fig. 1 shows the differences between the approaches and the relevant legal initiatives associated with them.

Scope and Legislation for Sustainability Reporting in the EU

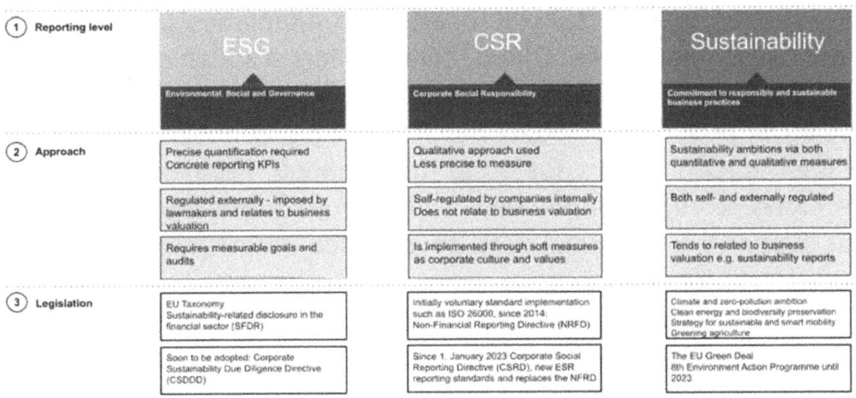

Fig. 1. Overview of the scope and relevant legislation for sustainability reporting in the European Union.

Source: Lutkevich (2023) and BaFin (2023).

Takeaways for CDOs outside the EU

- There is a competitive advantage in understanding EU business partners' needs and legally mandatory terms.
- It is important to know relevant legislation to prepare the home organization for the EU market.
- Preparatory work might be needed in dealing different jurisdictions in case the home country or other regions follow up with data protection and sustainability measures.

2.2. *Data Architecture*

Before delving into data sharing and the critical role of dataspaces in ESG reporting, we must understand the necessary IT infrastructures that are needed to prepare companies to participate in dataspaces. The first aspect is data storage at the company level. The way companies deal with their data indicates their data and technical maturity and provides an assessment of their level of readiness to participate in large-scale data-sharing initiatives.

As of today, companies use several ways of storing corporate data in a combination of local or on-premise storage and cloud storage, tailored to their specific needs and oftentimes prompted by historical developments. Cloud storage offers a suitable solution for data sharing: One reason is the accessibility and scalability of datasets as large amounts of data can be accessed from anywhere with an internet connection, fostering data sharing. Furthermore, modern cloud storage comes with a reliable data management layer that supports companies' data governance requirements and is a prerequisite for data sharing.

In recent years, the development and deployment of cloud-based applications have risen immensely, driven by attractive on-demand features and advantages for the industry and research community. Among cloud-based applications, cloud storage is the most successful one, as it manages to match the massive data-sharing demand effectively. Data only have to be uploaded to the cloud, and access rights have to be granted to the data sharer.

Cloud storage of corporate data in organizations worldwide 2015-2022

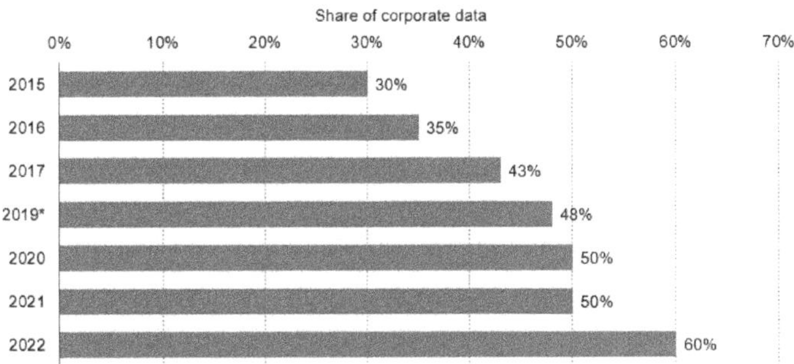

Fig. 2.   Share of corporate data stored in the cloud in organizations worldwide from 2015 to 2022.

Source: Statista (2022).

Once these are done, data sharers can obtain the data from the cloud instead of the data owner (Kumar *et al.*, 2018, p. 1). Due to the ease of use, cloud storage solutions have rapidly increased within the last decade as shown in Fig. 2 (Ponemon Institute & Thales Group, 2023).

These factors are important mainly because dataspace usage is based on two pillars: (1) technical infrastructure and (2) trust. The usage of cloud solutions can be seen as an indicator of both the level of data maturity of companies and their readiness and trust to confide their data in new digital technologies. The European non-profit Gaia-X Association states that the software required to implement dataspaces runs on the cloud/edge cloud infrastructure (Gaia-x, 2020). Dataspaces are founded on the principles of trust and relationships. Within such a dataspace, data governance is a core concept to facilitate these concepts through well-established rules and guidelines. Data governance streamlines the process to realize a community's vision: creating value by enabling seamless data discovery, access, interoperability, and reuse regardless of data location while ensuring trust and security (Curry *et al.*, 2022, p. 86).

The next step is the exchange of data between different data providers and users in a safe and compliant way while maintaining data sovereignty. Access to a broader database will be necessary to respond to the new upcoming reporting requirements for companies in the European Union.

2.3. *Technical and Public Landscape*

In the previous section, the basic company-level requirements for dataspaces to come to life were discussed. Dataspace is not storage but a trusted platform to exchange data. Hence, dataspace refers to a type of data relationship between trusted partners and provides high-level standards and guidelines for data storage and sharing within one or many data ecosystems (Gaia-x, 2020).

A dataspace is the sum of all its participants, consisting of data providers, users, and intermediaries. A critical and trust-enhancing advantage of the dataspace concept is that data are not stored centrally, but kept at their original source. Thus, they are only transferred through semantic interoperability with predefined necessary access rights and are kept exclusively by the participants. This conventionally requires the setting up of universally applicable technical architecture on an international level.

The German government funded a research project conducted by the Fraunhofer Institute for Software and System Technology on industrial dataspaces between April 2015 and April 2018 to explore technical requirements for intelligent data-sharing infrastructure models (FISS, 2018). The project resulted in the development of a reference architecture model. The International Data Spaces Association (IDSA), a founding member of the Gaia-X Association, has dedicated itself to co-creating the future of a global, digital economy by providing frameworks to manage data from different domains and regions within a global data ecosystem. It provides the reference architecture model to potential participants and helps them implement it. So far, this has been the only internationally certified and agreed-upon official framework for dataspaces. However, variations of the model are possible and functional, once approved and

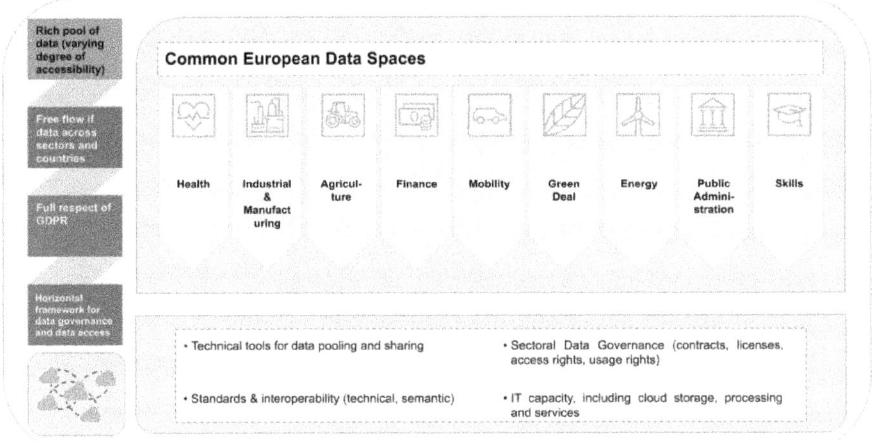

Fig. 3. Setup of the nine planned common European dataspaces.

Source: European Commission (2022b).

certified by the IDSA. The overall aim is to enable and stimulate the development of data value chains, retaining sovereignty and trustworthiness under European premises and values (Gaia-x, 2020).

Additionally, the European Commission has invested in the development of dataspaces that are of strategic importance for the growth of the European data economy.

Figure 3 visualizes the content of a staff working document from 2022 that presented nine common European dataspaces: Health, Industrial, Agriculture, Finance, Mobility, Green Deal, Energy, Public Administration, and Skills. However, the mere act might give the necessary direction but accompanying clarification on the objectives and essences of those dataspaces is required. These dataspaces might share common layers and concepts but will differ in sector-specific aspects.

3. Existing Obstacles for Dataspaces

As discussed, dataspaces provide the necessary infrastructure to enable the desired digital business activities and new data-based

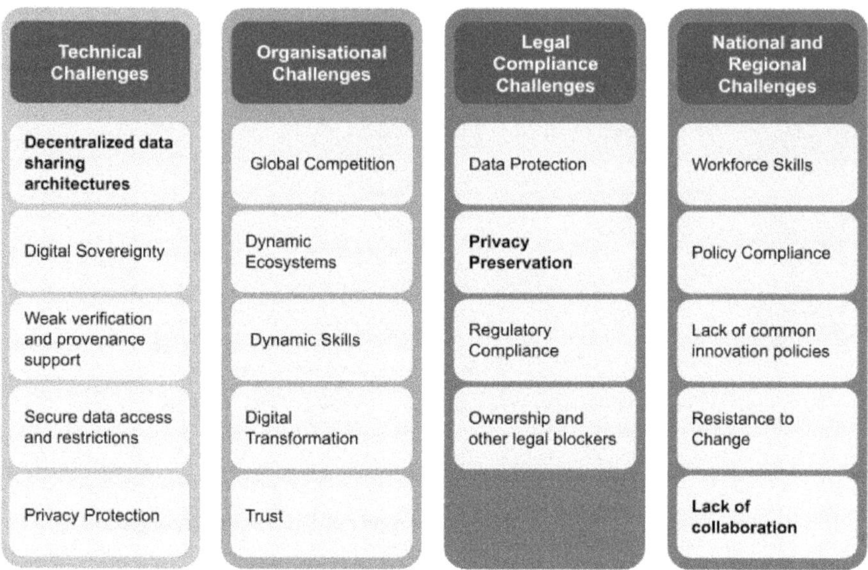

Fig. 4. Overview of different risk categories associated with using dataspaces. *Source*: Curry *et al.* (2022).

business models. In the data-driven landscape, the possibilities for and obstacles to sharing data emerge, necessitating a discussion for a more interconnected data environment.

Barriers to data sharing can be divided into various subcategories, such as "technical, organisational, legal compliance and regional/national challenges" (Curry *et al.*, 2022, p. 351). Figure 4 provides an overview of these obstacles:

In this section, the challenges specified in Fig. 4 in bold are discussed in greater detail.

One of the main challenges is decentralization or more specifically the issues resulting from the *interoperability of data formats* (Lasmaries, 2023). Each contributor might have different data structures, standards, and storage, leading to difficulties in exchanging and integrating information seamlessly. As a result of this heterogeneity, it is time-consuming and difficult to interpret data consistently across other dataspaces. "What is needed though is a comprehensive architecture of standards which includes different types of data such as master data, reference data, manufacturing and supply chain event data etc." (Kembuegler, 2020). An individual ecosystem member cannot develop this architecture stack but requires consensus within a community of practice.

According to the European Commission's "Study on data sharing between companies in Europe," *privacy concerns* are the principal barrier to business-to-business (B2B) data sharing (European Commission & everis Benelux, 2018). Hence, establishing clear security policies is essential to ensure compliance with personal data protection, user privacy regulations, and sensitive industry-specific data. In Europe, the EU's data strategy aims to enable data sharing and develop clear data access rules. Hence, two key policy measures, the Data Governance Act and the Data Act, are being advanced in the legislative process to encourage B2B data sharing while ensuring data sovereignty and security in international dataspaces (Swabey, 2021).

Lastly, *private and public sector collaboration* needs to be improved, as they have different priorities and interests regarding data sharing. Moreover, data-sharing collaboration between the private and public sectors is lacking due to data undervaluation, limited public sector expertise, insufficient incentives for private sector data sharing, professional shortages, legal disparities, trust, security, ethics, and data interoperability, leading to prolonged and uncertain processes (European Commission, 2022c). The EU can foster such collaboration by establishing a common framework and putting in place the technical infrastructure to share data and ethical guidelines while raising awareness about the potential of data sharing.

Despite the barriers involved in data exchange within dataspaces, it is essential to note that the opportunities outweigh the concerns. In the upcoming section, we will showcase successful examples of dataspaces in use.

Takeaways for CDOs outside the EU

- Understand the opportunities of dataspaces as platforms for collaboration.
- Dataspaces provide a suitable concept that enables data sharing within a robust framework built on trust.
- Joining a first-mover circle of business parties working with dataspaces grows your network, helping you get in touch with other CDOs.
- Prepare your company for new ways of market interaction.
- Helping EU business partners fulfill their reporting obligations will make you stand out from your competitors.
- Get insights into operation modes and learn best practices in data work.

4. Use Cases

The developments leading to these use cases have been described in the previous sections. The heavy regulations and technical frameworks may appear complex at first glance but have been adopted over the few past decades by companies and institutions operating in the European business environment. Hence, implementing these requirements also leads to opportunities for companies in these markets.

"Although private sector organisations are pursuing data sharing, successful real-world examples are sparse due to a multitude of barriers" (Fassnacht *et al.*, 2019). As outlined in the previous chapter, several challenges remain in bringing dataspaces to life. Nevertheless, some specific dataspaces have already been successfully established in the EU, adding significant value to European businesses. We want to shed light on positive examples of functioning data -haring models and show their implications for non-EU third parties working with EU-based companies.

4.1. *Mobility*

A rather prominent positive example is the Mobility Dataspace that serves as an open data ecosystem to facilitate the storage and exchange of mobility and traffic data.

Within the Mobility Dataspace (see Fig. 5), various stakeholders in the transportation sector act as both data requesters and data providers, retaining full autonomy and control of the utilization of their data by third parties. Through this approach, a high level of data sovereignty as well as trust is fostered, leading to genuine economic value and business incentives. Sensitive and protected data can therefore be used and shared safely under the conditions set by the data providers, ensuring data quality and transparency about the origin for data users (Otto *et al.*, 2022, p. 350).

"Whilst mobility brings many benefits for its users, it is not without costs for our society" (EUMonitor, 2020). The convenience of private and public transportation undoubtedly improved day-to-day life and business opportunities in society. However, the mobility sector faces a set of challenges regarding its negative environmental and social impacts that need to be addressed.

While increasing attention is placed on greenhouse gas emissions caused by modes of transportation, the core issue in the mobility sector runs much deeper. To truly take an effective step toward sustainability and the protection of human rights in the mobility sector, it is essential to consider the entire supply chain of the mobility industry in terms of meeting ESG and due diligence requirements.

To enhance the efficiency and safety of mobility and transportation while also fostering better monitoring and protection of human rights and the environment, collecting and sharing large amounts of mobility data, such as real-time data on the traffic and traffic infrastructure, are very important (Otto *et al.*, 2022, p. 344). Hence, a common mobility dataspace is needed that pools data from public and private services and sources, enabling the exchange and

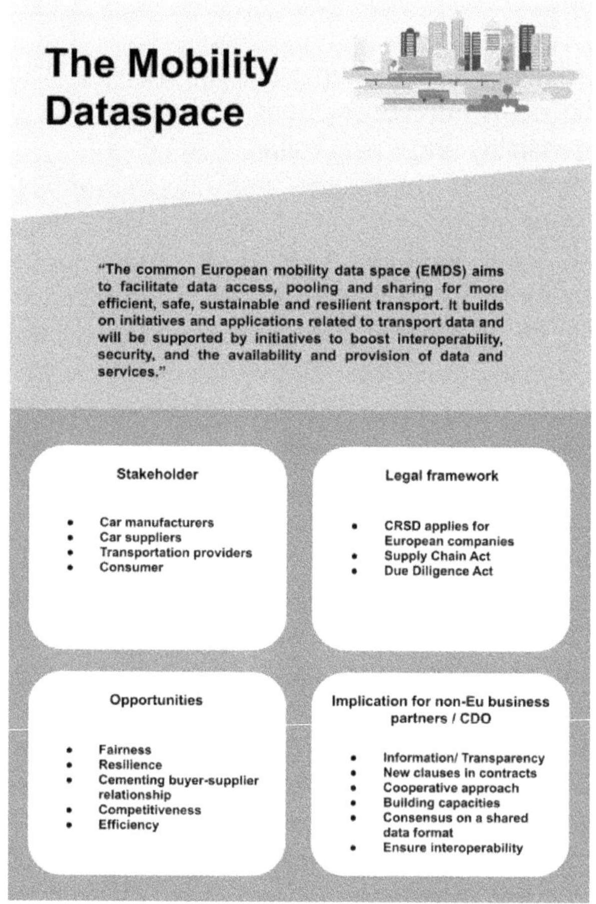

Fig. 5. Overview of the common mobility dataspace.

Source: European Commission (2023) and Federal Ministry for Economic Cooperation and Development (BMZ) Division Sustainable Transformation of Global Supply Chains (2023).

usage of sensitive and protected data and building the infrastructure for more efficient and sustainable mobility.

4.2. *Healthcare*

EU ESG reporting responsibilities also apply to the healthcare sector. This includes saving resources, avoiding waste, and reducing energy-related CO_2 emissions (PwC US, n.d.). Moreover, mandatory ESG reporting regulations now require hospitals to disclose sustainability data (Envoria, 2023), highlighting the importance of efficient data collection and data usage. Thus, healthcare leaders can use proven tactics and smarter technologies to identify specifications, measure data, and hold their businesses accountable to ESG principles.

However, upon a closer look at the healthcare sector, disparities characterize its digitalization and data management. These will impact the speed with which data can be shared within this field. An example of the disparity in digital technology usage between departments and participating parties is as follows: Departments such as radiology use advanced AI tools for image analysis, whereas resident physicians sometimes still use outdated methods like faxing. Moreover, "Patients use their smartwatch to record ECGs, while their doctor records blood pressure in a paper file" (Otto *et al.*, 2022, p. 291). However, as mentioned in Section 2.2, digital workflows require harmonized processes and data structures, leading to obstacles in data sharing within organizations in this specific domain.

This shows that in the healthcare domain, providers lack an exemplary data infrastructure, and therefore struggle to share patients' vital data effectively. One reason is the heterogeneity in both the nature of healthcare providers (e.g., hospitals, laboratories, or pharmaceutical producers) and their data usage, as well as the lack of regulations regarding data sharing. The collection of high-quality and sizable datasets to advance precision medicine is therefore a challenging task. Finally, medical data are the most sensitive type of data and are subject to strict privacy policies. Sensitivity restrictions imply, for example, that only authorized personnel such as doctors and medical experts are allowed to access this kind of information, not necessarily data engineers and developers who could further develop the datasets.

The scattered landscape in the healthcare field represents a big challenge that cannot be overcome through the implementation of a single type of data infrastructure. Organizations need common incentives and regulations from the ecosystem to foster a sustainable data-sharing foundation (Otto *et al.*, 2022, p. 292).

Nevertheless, regardless of obstacles, there are also successful data-sharing projects in this highly important and promising field, one of which is the online Clinical Study Data Request (CSDR) platform with ideaPoint being the technical third-party provider (ideaPoint, 2023). The provider handles all the before-mentioned obstacles and still realizes data sharing on its platform. It provides registered researchers and other companies with access to patient-level clinical trial data from 14 leading pharmaceutical organizations (Lindner *et al.*, 2021). More than 3,500 clinical trials can be accessed through this platform, enabling users to improve their working efficiency (ideaPoint, 2023).

On the one hand, the interoperability issue of data formats is solved due to standardized data formats within this platform (see Fig. 6). On the other hand, data and information are carefully selected, ensuring high-quality standards of datasets, while data use agreements and strict policies foster data security and privacy preservation. In summary, CSDR is a successful trailblazer data-sharing platform that can be seen as a positive impetus for other European companies to invest in data-friendly constructs.

5. Value Creation Opportunities for CDOs

In the last section of this chapter, we will state the implications and opportunities for CDOs amid many complex developments. We have shown that European regulation has a major impact on stakeholders and countries outside of Europe. However, this does not need to be seen in a necessarily negative light.

CDOs have the advantage of holding a unique role that interfaces with different departments and fields that are essential for smooth business functioning. Hence, CDOs need to stay ahead of different topics and keep an eye on data-related developments in the field in which their company operates. New regulations and requirements may affect the way business operates with data, both in their domiciled location and abroad. Contrary to traditional

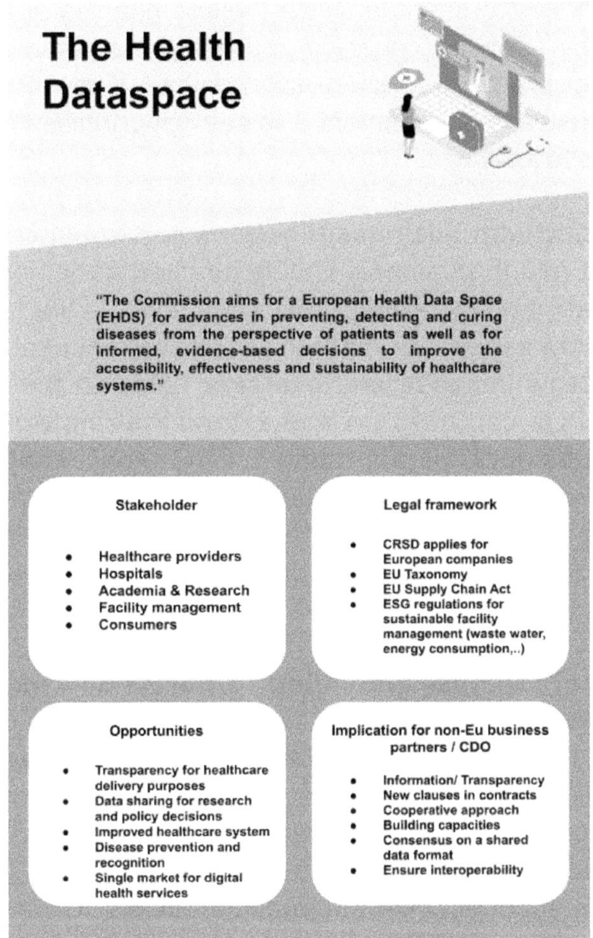

Fig. 6. Overview of the health dataspace.

departments such as the legal or IT, the CDO does not have a merely one-sided or predefined approach but is in a horizontal position with an overarching and holistic view. As such, CDOs can assess the implications of new developments in the respective business fields.

Therefore, Chief Data Officers hold a central position to guide the company through various requirements and influences shaping the business environment in which their companies operate. They can do so by adopting coherent and fitting data governance and management practices to brace companies for new challenges in the digital business environment. We see opportunities for CDOs in terms of the following:

- **Interfacing with business functions and connecting people**
As a hybrid role in business, CDOs function as an intermediary both internally and externally. This can be within the firm, assisting in the data aspects of different business functions and identifying strategic linkages and overlaps between them. Outside the firm, CDOs can build on and extend their network with relevant stakeholders for appropriate ESG work, enabling interconnectedness and the flow of information. In this way, they can prepare the organization to conduct business with third parties in other countries with different underlying restrictions and regulations.

- **Technical expertise and fitting corporate data management practices**
An opportunity for CDOs also lies in their day-to-day business: Understanding new challenges and requirements helps the CDO adapt the corporate data management strategy and guide the firm's data setup in times of change. CDOs can also align with their counterparts such as Chief Information Officers (CIOs) and Chief Technology Officers (CTOs) to introduce promising and quality-enhancing technologies that will help the company stay competitive and ahead of new trends and obligations, for example, by introducing or developing a tailored ESG reporting software.

- **An esteemed partner for assistance in strategic decisions-making**
CDOs provide valuable guidance on transnational and international data-related developments both from the technical, and business aspects and they can also provide assistance with their holistic point of view when it comes to long-term strategic decisions-making for the company.

- **Development of new business models and data products/ services**

In the major area that is corporate data, one of the key responsibilities of a CDO is utilizing existing data within and sharing it through dataspaces, creating an ongoing chance to increase the value of company assets. In this way, on the one hand, CDOs can help improve efficiency in operations by identifying development opportunities and acquiring external data in a structured, strategic, and pragmatic manner to reduce risk and further the business. On the other hand, new data products and services can be created using existing datasets in a compliant way.

- **Support digital upskilling and data culture**

Bringing data and information closer to the employees helps to showcase immediate and long-term value through data and digital products. This helps overcome possible reservations toward the active use of data and technology that will prevent a company from tapping into its full potential and efficiency with data and meeting data-related requirements such as ESG reporting and ESG conformity of business plans.

Figure 7 provides an overview of the opportunities arising from extended data collection for ESG purposes for CDOs.

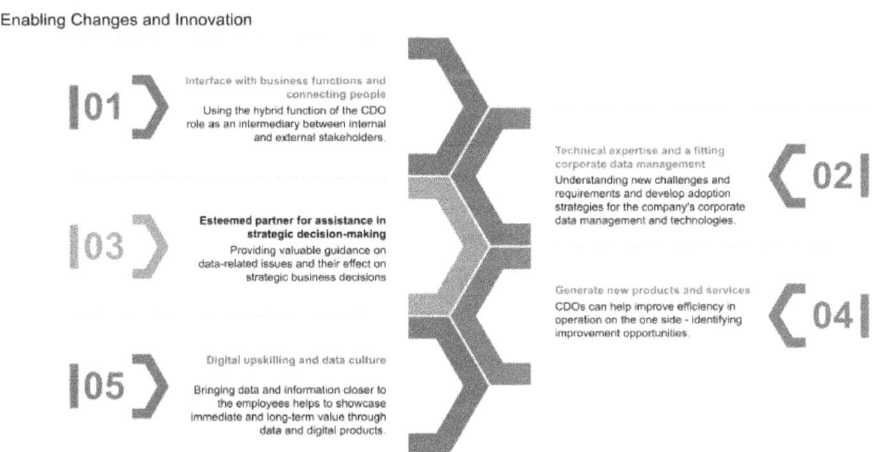

Fig. 7.   Opportunities that Come with ESG for Chief Data Officers.

Takeaways for CDOs outside the EU

- Use the CDO position as an interface between strategic and technical topics.
- Become an advisor on strategic decision-making with a global view on the environment the company operates in and is affected by.
- Leveraging the knowledge on different topics will help demonstrate the importance of your role and push your tasks to C-level visibility.
- Learn from other companies and markets by gaining insights into best practices in data work.
- Create transparency with data with regard to the processes of a company, thereby enhancing trust and getting a better overview, which also benefits self-improvement.

---

6. Summary

In conclusion, this chapter has emphasized the growing significance of not only technical but also sustainability and ESG considerations within the European business environment, majorly driven by initiatives such as the EU "Green Deal." Measuring sustainability efforts can only be done with proper ESG reporting. As in many fields of today and in the future, data lie at the heart of such ambitions — with measurement, collection, sharing, and analysis. The EU has recognized this development, charted in the European Data Strategy to harness high-quality data for innovation and progress. Central to this journey are the Corporate Sustainability Reporting Directive (CSRD) standards, implemented to strengthen data-driven ESG reporting.

After the introduction, we discussed the role of data architecture, which represents the foundation of data sharing. Within this narrative, cloud storage solutions gain importance in different domains and the use of dataspaces can be seen as a maturity indicator. Dataspaces are fostering efficient data sharing across and within organizations and are build on the premise of accessibility and scalability of use.

However, along with data sharing, challenges arise — from format interoperability to data privacy to the lack of collaboration between the public and private sectors. Despite these obstacles, use cases of successful data sharing have emerged, which are politically desired by the European Union. The European Union has communicated the foundation of nine industry and sector-specific common European dataspaces. These dataspaces will ensure high-quality and safe data sharing within the EU. So far, in practice, a few smaller dataspaces have been established and used for ESG-related data sharing, illustrating how dataspaces can be harnessed effectively. Examples of functioning dataspace were illustrated in the mobility and health sectors, leading to diverse environment analysis and data-sharing implementations.

In the final section, we highlighted the opportunities arising from these technical and sustainability-driven developments for CDOs in organizations. CDOs provide the compass for strategic decisions, guide new business models, and cultivate the data culture for organizations. CDOs have a fundamental role in implementing strong data management, enabling the organization to measure and use data more effectively, especially in essential missions required by law such as ESG reporting. A successful CDO can and must leverage existing and upcoming regulations to lead their enterprise into a truly data-driven organization. These regulatory changes must be interpreted and communicated by the CDO with value-enriching emphasis leading to a comprehensive data vision.

In essence, the journey we have undertaken in this chapter illustrates the evolving business landscape in Europe and advocates for CDOs to embrace the opportunities data management provides for businesses. This chapter emphasizes the importance of data in ESG, the transformative potential of dataspaces, and the essential role of the CDO. As a parting thought, we would recommend that CDOs leverage existing challenges and requirements that stem from regulatory pressure to facilitate internal discussions, build the data infrastructure, and envision bigger and more innovative concepts that will add value to their company sustainably.

References

BaFin. (2023, March 8). The EU sustainable finance disclosure regulation: Opening the door to greater transparency. BaFin. Retrieved October 25, 2023, from https://www.bafin.de/SharedDocs/Veroeffentlichungen/EN/Fachartikel/2022/fa_bj_2212_Offenlegungsverordnung_en.html.

Beyrouthy, L. (2023, August 16). Europe: e-commerce revenue 2018-2027. *Statista*. Retrieved October 10, 2023, from https://www.statista.com/forecasts/715663/e-commerce-revenue-forecast-in-europe.

Curry, E., Scerri, S., and Tuikka, T. (eds.). (2022). *Data Spaces: Design, Deployment and Future Directions*. Cham: Springer International Publishing. https://link.springer.com/book/10.1007/978-3-030-98636-0.

Envoria. (2023, August 10). Sustainability reporting in healthcare and hospitals. Envoria. Retrieved October 26, 2023, from https://envoria.com/insights-news/esg-reporting-in-hospitals-and-clinics.

EUMonitor. (2020, December 9). Legal provisions of COM(2020)789 — Sustainable and smart mobility strategy — Putting European transport on track for the future. EUMonitor. Retrieved October 24, 2023, from https://www.eumonitor.eu/9353000/1/j4nvhdfcs8bljza_j9vvik7m1c3gyxp/vlehreuol0wv.

European Commission. (2019a). The European green deal. European Commission. Retrieved October 10, 2023, from https://commission.europa.eu/strategy-and-policy/priorities-2019-2024/european-green-deal_en.

European Commission. (2019b). Europe's digital decade: Digital targets for 2030. European Commission. Retrieved October 10, 2023, from https://commission.europa.eu/strategy-and-policy/priorities-2019-2024/europe-fit-digital-age/europes-digital-decade-digital-targets-2030_en.

European Commission. (2020, February 19). Communication from the commission to the European parliament, the council, the European economic and social committee and the committee of the regions. EUR-Lex. Retrieved October 23, 2023, from https://eur-lex.europa.eu/legal-content/EN/TXT/PDF/?uri=CELEX:52020DC0066.

European Commission. (2022a, August 17). Business-to-government data sharing: Questions and answers. Shaping Europe's digital future. Retrieved October 11, 2023, from https://digital-strategy.ec.europa.eu/en/faqs/business-government-data-sharing-questions-and-answers.

European Commission. (2022b, February 23). Commission Staff Working Document on Common European Data Spaces. Brussels, Belgium. Retrieved

October 24, 2023, from https://digital-strategy.ec.europa.eu/en/library/staff-working-document-data-spaces.

European Commission. (2022c). Digitalisation of Businesses: A Guide to EU Funding Opportunities. Publications Office of the European Union, p. 12. 10.2759/931100.

European Commission. (2023). Transport data — creating a common European mobility data space (communication). Initiative details. Retrieved October 26, 2023, from https://ec.europa.eu/info/law/better-regulation/have-your-say/initiatives/13566-Transport-data-creating-a-common-European-mobility-data-space-communication-_en.

European Commission & everis Benelux. (2018, April 24). Study on Data Sharing between Companies in Europe: Final Report. Publications Office. Retrieved October 11, 2023, from https://op.europa.eu/en/publication-detail/-/publication/8b8776ff-4834-11e8-be1d-01aa75ed71a1/language-en.

Fassnacht, M. K., *et al.* (2019, March 9). Barriers to data sharing among private sector organizations. YouTube. Retrieved October 11, 2023, from https://publikationen.bibliothek.kit.edu/1000150870.

Federal Ministry for Economic Cooperation and Development (BMZ) Division Sustainable Transformation of Global Supply Chains. (2023). The German act on corporate due diligence obligations in supply chains. bmz.de. https://www.bmz.de/resource/blob/154774/lieferkettengesetz-faktenpapier-partnerlaender-eng-bf.pdf.

Federal Ministry of Labour and Social Affairs. (2023, June 15). CSR — EU supply chain law initiative. CSR-in-Deutschland.de. Retrieved October 25, 2023, from https://www.csr-in-deutschland.de/EN/Business-Human-Rights/Europe/EU-supply-chain-law-initiative/eu-supply-chain-law-initiative.html.

FISS. (2018). Leitprojekte/Initiativen — International Data spaces. Fraunhofer-Gesellschaft. Retrieved October 10, 2023, from https://www.fraunhofer.de/de/forschung/fraunhofer-initiativen/international-data-spaces.html#2.

Gaia-x. (2020). Data spaces. Gaia-X. Retrieved October 18, 2023, from https://gaia-x.eu/what-is-gaia-x/deliverables/data-spaces/.

ideaPoint. (2023). ClinicalStudyDataRequest.com. Retrieved October 24, 2023, from https://www.clinicalstudydatarequest.com/.

Kembuegler. (2020, March 9). Data sharing in industrial ecosystems (part 3 of 4). International Data Spaces. Retrieved October 11, 2023, from https://internationaldataspaces.org/data-sharing-in-industrial-ecosystems-part-3-of-4/.

Kumar, R., Porselvan, G., Kumar, S. P., and Robinlash, F. (2018, January). Security and privacy based data sharing in cloud computing. *Engineering & Management (IJIREM)* 5(1), 5. DOI: 10.21276/ijirem.2018.5.1.9.

Lasmaries, E. (2023, July 12). Challenges and opportunities of data exchange through data spaces. Visions. Retrieved October 11, 2023, from https://

visionspol.eu/en/2023/07/12/challenges-and-opportunities-of-data-exchange-through-data-spaces/.

Lindner, M., Straub, LL. M. S., and Kühne, D. B. (2021, April). How to share data? Data sharing platforms for organizations. Digitale Technologien. Retrieved October 24, 2023, from https://www.digitale-technologien.de/DT/Redaktion/EN/Downloads/Publikation/smartdata_%20Datasharing.pdf?__blob=publicationFile&v=1.

Lutkevich, B. (2023, April 21). ESG vs. CSR vs. sustainability: What's the difference? TechTarget. Retrieved October 25, 2023, from https://www.techtarget.com/whatis/feature/ESG-vs-CSR-vs-sustainability-Whats-the-difference.

Mobility Data Space. (2022). In: Otto, B., ten Hompel, M., and Wrobel, S. (eds.), *Designing Data Spaces: The Ecosystem Approach to Competitive Advantage*. Cham: Springer International Publishing, pp. 343–361. https://link.springer.com/chapter/10.1007/978-3-030-93975-5_21.

Otto, B., ten Hompel, M., and Wrobel, S. (eds.). (2022). *Designing Data Spaces: The Ecosystem Approach to Competitive Advantage*. Cham: Springer International Publishing. https://link.springer.com/book/10.1007/978-3-030-93975-5.

Ponemon Institute & Thales Group. (2023, September 28). Share of corporate data stored in the cloud in organizations worldwide from 2015 to 2022 [Graph]. *Statista*. Retrieved October 16, 2023, from https://www.statista.com/statistics/1062879/worldwide-cloud-storage-of-corporate-data/.

PwC US. (n.d.). How health organizations can integrate ESG priorities. PwC. Retrieved October 24, 2023, from https://www.pwc.com/us/en/industries/health-industries/library/esg-health-industry.html.

Schmit, N. (2023, July 6). Report finds labour and skills shortages persist. European Commission. Retrieved October 10, 2023, from https://ec.europa.eu/commission/presscorner/detail/en/ip_23_3704.

Swabey, P. (2021, September 27). Data spaces and beyond: the future of b2b data sharing. Tech Monitor. Retrieved October 11, 2023, from https://techmonitor.ai/policy/digital-economy/policymakers-want-businesses-to-share-more-data-how-might-it-work.

YouGov. (2022). Junges Europa 2023. TUI Stiftung. Retrieved October 10, 2023, from https://www.tui-stiftung.de/wp-content/uploads/2023/06/2023_06_02-YouGov_Ergebnisbericht_TUI-Stiftung_Junges-Europa.pdf.

Chapter 8

Overview — AI Value Creation

Dr Thara Ravindran

*Research Fellow, Nanyang Business School,
NTU Singapore
rthara@ntu.edu.sg*

We are currently witnessing a global Artificial intelligence (AI) revolution termed the "AI Spring" wherein organizations are scrambling to adopt and experiment with AI to transform their processes and services and realize business value. According to reports, in the last 5 years, there has been a doubling of AI adoption among organizations worldwide. The early adopters who have tasted success continue their experimentation and have since accelerated the pace, forging ahead with their AI-driven strategies. More and more organizations have reported the use of tools such as Robotic Process Automation (RPA), computer vision, natural language processing, virtual agents and interfaces, recommender systems, facial recognition, robotics, and generative AI.

AI has been touted as the most disruptive emergent technology of the coming decade, that wields the power to enable the creation of enormous value for all types of businesses.

1. How Exactly Does AI Enable Value Creation?

Undoubtedly, the answer lies in AI's ability to adopt intelligent behavior, automate processes, and perform complex problem-solving. The enhanced data processing capabilities of AI and the ability to change its behavior based on user input make this suite of technologies valuable for organizations looking to improve operational efficiencies and develop a powerful competitive edge. AI also accelerates innovation by helping firms to derive insights from large datasets and predicting unexpected events. Artificial intelligence (AI) allows easy access and exchange of information and knowledge between business partners, further strengthening strategic links. Firms are now empowered to create additional value by adopting a proactive approach, managing uncertainties and unexpected events, as well as identifying and exploiting new opportunities, thereby improving efficiencies and increasing revenue.

The most common use cases reported have been in service operations, new products and services, customer segmentation and acquisition, lead generation, and customer service. Now, this leaves room for many more interesting use cases supported by emerging AI technologies to evolve and transform businesses in the near future. Needless to say, businesses have reported higher perceived value in investing in AI and they are justified in their optimism. However, despite all this good news, according to a 2022 McKinsey report,[1] the proportion of organizations adopting AI has plateaued at 50–60% during the 5 years leading up to 2022. This points to the hidden challenges in AI adoption that can potentially hinder its effective exploitation within an enterprise.

2. Challenges Ahead

Various categories of generic AI risks have come to light over years of experimentation and research: Some of these are related to the design of AI systems, including cybersecurity, personal privacy, explainability, equity and fairness, and physical safety, whereas

---

[1] https://www.mckinsey.com/capabilities/quantumblack/our-insights/the-state-of-ai-in-2022-and-a-half-decade-in-review.

others include aspects that have an impact at an organizational or even national level, such as workforce/labor displacement, regulatory compliance, organizational reputation, national security, and political stability. The fact that there has not been a proportionate increase in the number of firms recognizing these known AI risks as relevant and pledging adequate investments in mitigating them raises concerns.

As such, this would be an appropriate time to assess the value that AI can deliver to firms, while at the same time developing a deeper understanding of the generic issues that would hinder the optimal and realistic exploitation of AI capabilities.

3. Chapters on AI Value Creation

It is in this context that we present this section on AI value generation that includes a collection of five chapters addressing the following themes: (1) A survey of AI and its impact on the digital ecosystem to provide an overview of the capabilities and issues surrounding this suite of technologies. (2) How do we use Gen AI to create value? (3) What are some of the best practices firms can adopt to ensure value creation? (4) What are the practical lessons in AI implementation for value creation? (5) What are some of the legal/copyright implications of Gen AI adoption?

Selected authors have contributed the following chapters that showcase how AI can realize value in various business contexts and highlight the challenges that arise in the course of AI implementation:

Chapter 10: N. Chew (2024) The Rise of Artificial Intelligence;

Chapter 11: S. Tonk (2024) Generative AI for Advanced Value Creation;

Chapter 12: M. Taylor (2024) Tipping the Scales with AI: Harnessing Data and AI to Enhance Business Value;

Chapter 13: C. Asavathiratham (2024) Using AI to Power a Digital Bank with a Human Touch;

Chapter 14: H. Y.-F. Lim (2024) Generative AI Output for Business Organizations: Legal Perspectives from Copyright Law.

An introduction to AI capabilities and the suite of applications that fall under the gamut of AI is provided by Neumann Chew. The objective is to ensure a fundamental understanding of AI and the impact of this suite of technologies on day-to-day lives and business ecosystems. This provides a context for an appreciation and understanding of the subsequent chapters in this section.

In recent years, generative AI (Gen AI), a type of AI technology that is capable of generating high-quality text, images, audio, and synthetic data from existing content, has raised the expectations of users and businesses alike. Sachin Tonk's chapter presents an overview of the current state of generative AI and its potential impact on the digital ecosystem. It also covers recent advancements in Gen AI, illustrating how this spurs creativity and facilitates problem-solving in innovative ways besides channeling the use of AI into uncharted territories. Novel applications of Gen AI ranging from application in art generation to drug discovery to election campaigning have been reported, raking up ethical and legal concerns from various quarters. While these rapid developments continue to raise questions, there is no denying the endless possibilities they open up as Gen AI redefines service paradigms and extends a promise to improve human lives. Sachin's chapter provides a glimpse into these aspects or the "what" of Gen AI, thereby underlining the need for firms to understand and exploit this suite of technologies to engage with data in innovative ways.

As we traverse a frenzied phase of development of any emerging technology, pressing questions about how to go about its implementation arise. The next three chapters in this section, therefore, will investigate the "how" of AI implementation for value creation. Michael Taylor's chapter discusses issues surrounding the implementation of AI-based solutions. How can organizations implement AI ensuring some level of success and addressing known risks? What tools and techniques are available to help operationalize data and AI programs? What are the resource requirements? What are the ways in which AI can fail and how can these failures be avoided?

Bearing these questions in mind, Michael Taylor's chapter shares some best practices distilled from successful AI projects that can guide organizations through the process of executing AI projects. We hope that this chapter will guide data leaders toward strategizing with AI and data, democratizing their use by empowering users at all levels, besides strengthening the data-to-insight-to-action loop by ensuring that AI is harnessed for identifying actionable items to yield stronger business results.

Chalee Asavathiratham, the Chief Digital Banking Officer at Siam Commercial Bank, shares the story of the bank's journey toward transforming itself from a traditional establishment into a digital entity by blending AI capabilities with a "human touch." This is an interesting case of how a service-based organization harnessed the power of AI and the "undigitizable" aspects of banking services typically offered by human agents to provide a unique customer service experience. In this chapter, Chalee takes us through the bank's transition to a hybrid AI–human service model, which has helped to differentiate it from the other banks in the region. The lessons distilled from this case are sure to inspire and guide other similar organizations toward implementing AI-based business strategies successfully.

With the looming number of copyright litigations filed internationally over the acquisition and use of content for training AI systems, there has been an increased awareness of this somewhat murky area in recent times. Digital content creators such as writers, artists, and musicians have been threatened by the risk of unauthorized access and use of their copyrighted content by AI systems. Numerous events have come to light in recent years that have focused on the issue surrounding the working of Gen AI. On December 27, 2023, *The New York Times* filed a law suit against Open AI and Microsoft over their use of millions of its articles without permission for training their AI systems.

Against this backdrop, Prof. Yee Fen Lim's chapter presents a critical analysis of the legal landscape of generative AI and its implications for businesses. Several important questions have been addressed in this chapter including: How can AI generated raw outputs be protected under copyright law? How can these raw outputs be redesigned so that they can be turned into protected creative assets for firms? Copyright legislation that would allow protection for computer-generated works without a human creator has been cited, as also interesting litigations involving such works. The aim is to ensure that AI is harnessed within the boundaries defined by the legal framework so that strategic business leaders are able to minimize exposure to legal risks and liabilities arising out of the use of generative AI.

In summary, the chapters in this section have been carefully put together to provide the reader with a high-level understanding of the important pieces of the AI jigsaw that we trust would offer guidance for organizations looking to implement AI within their respective work environments.

Chapter 9

The Rise of Artificial Intelligence

C. H. Neumann Chew

*Nanyang Business School, NTU Singapore.
91 Nanyang Avenue, Academic Building South (Gaia),
#06-18, Singapore 639956
neumann.chew@ntu.edu.sg*

Abstract

We review the rise of Artificial Intelligence (AI), explaining the unique characteristics of different variants of AI, where they were successfully applied, their strengths and weaknesses, and where they spectacularly failed. The role of human judgment and oversight is critical and still necessary in the current stage of AI until the day AI can govern itself and correct mistakes on its own.

Keywords: Machine learning, supervised learning, unsupervised learning, neural networks, random forests, classification and regression trees (CART), text mining, ChatGPT.

1. The Test of Intelligence in Machines

World War II was a war of human intellect, willpower, and computing power. The massive towers of computing machines were critical for the decryption of enemies' messages. The tireless computations, guided by human masters, proved their value. Shortly after the end of the war, researchers continued working to enhance computing machines and many started exploring the idea of intelligence in machines. The key question is it possible to construct intelligent machines?

Several ideas to define intelligence in machines were proposed, and eventually, Alan Turing's idea prevailed in 1950. Intelligence in machines can be objectively tested and the Turing Test shows how the test can be done (Fig. 1).

A computer (entity A) and a human (entity B) are behind closed doors and receive typed questions from another human (entity C). C reviews the typed responses from both A and B. After several rounds of "conversation," C must declare which of the two entities is a human (and the other a computer). If A manages to make C think that it is a human responding, then A is deemed to be intelligent. Since A is in reality a machine, it can be considered Artificial Intelligence (AI).

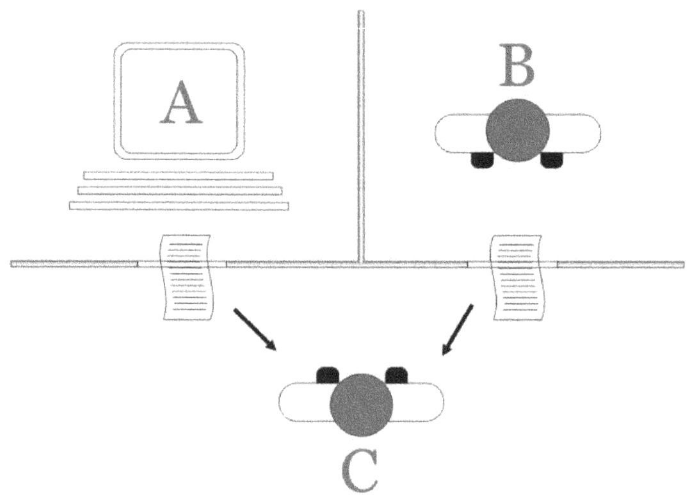

Fig. 1.   The Turing test.

Source: https://en.wikipedia.org/wiki/Turing_test.

Alan Turing's idea of intelligence in machines prevailed mainly because it is testable. However, there are several limitations. Firstly, the test is based on the ability to trick another human. This is not a necessary condition as honest entities can be intelligent too. Secondly, the test is based on human conversations. This is also not a necessary condition as entities can demonstrate intelligence without conversations. Thirdly, the test is based on human likeness. To pass the test, entity A's replies must seem like those of a human. If the replies are too outstanding, super-human-like, or too intelligent to be human, then A would fail the test and be deemed not intelligent — an oxymoron to the term intelligent.

A second group of researchers started to pursue a different pathway to achieving intelligence that did not require trickery, human conversation, or human likeness. This is now known as machine learning.

2. The Machine Learning Branch of AI

Machine learning seeks to automatically learn from data and improve on specific tasks without being explicitly programmed. The focus is on improving performance on specific tasks (e.g., winning elections, predicting diseases, forecasting stock prices, or purchasing a recommended product) automatically with data. This criterion is very practical and useful and has found ubiquitous applications in all modern societies. Successful machine learning applications (Chew, 2021) include the following:

- Movie Recommendation Systems,
- Heart Attack Prognosis,
- Cancer Diagnosis based on Digital Images,
- Predictive Asset Maintenance,
- Optimized Scheduling,
- Fraud Detection,
- Bank Loan Approvals,
- Emergency Room Triage and Waiting Times.

In a movie recommendation system, the machine learning algorithm learns the likes and dislikes of each customer profile and computes the probability of customers liking a new movie. The customers who were predicted to love a new movie are then sent the recommendation. This is the basis for Netflix's rise from a start-up to a multimillion-dollar company.

Heart attack prognosis is difficult without timely blood test results. The patient profile together with non-invasive indicators (blood pressure, heart rate, temperature, etc.) forms the dataset fed into a machine learning algorithm to predict the prognosis. The accuracy is good enough to be used in the hospital emergency departments.[1]

Cancer diagnosis can be made from MRI scans and other digital images. However, some hospitals have insufficient radiologists to interpret the images. Machine learning algorithms have been applied to predict cancer from digital images with high accuracy.[2]

Essential equipment is known to fail occasionally (trains, lifts, production lines, oil drilling, etc.). By collecting sensor data, machine learning algorithms can be trained to learn the patterns of equipment vibration before imminent failure so as to predict the failure and more importantly pinpoint the exact location of the failure so that just-in-time servicing can be activated to prevent equipment malfunction.

Resources (humans, equipment, rooms, etc.) can be scheduled or priced more optimally if one can predict demand accurately. Machine learning algorithms have proven to be superior to time series forecasting models if relevant demand parameter data can be provided.

Fraud detection machine learning algorithms have been used to risk-score applications offline (loan applications, insurance applications, etc.) and in real time (credit card transactions, interbank fund transfer, etc.). The accuracy depends on the false-positive vs false-negative trade-off desired by the company. The imbalanced

---

[1] See Breiman *et al.* (1983).
[2] See Street *et al.* (1993).

data problem needs to be addressed as part of data preparation before feeding the data into the machine learning algorithm. This is a prevalent problem in rare-event prediction and is highly resistant to attempts to improve the accuracy. Instead of optimizing models, it is faster and often more effective to prepare a more balanced trainset instead.

Typically, banks receive a lot of bank loan applications (retail and corporate). Machine learning algorithms are commonly used to risk-score and reject/approve each application. Data are provided in the application form and the credit score is maintained by an independent organization.

At an emergency department, nurses record patient symptoms and readings. For non-obvious cases, patients will be risk-scored by an algorithm that learns from historical patient data to determine how long the patient can wait to see a doctor.

The success of machine learning is determined by three key factors: (1) predictive need, (2) imperfect knowledge, and (3) availability of data. The predictive task needs to originate from an essential business need. Netflix needs to know which customers in their database are likely to love a new movie just released; a hospital needs to know what is the disease or prognosis so as to give the right treatment; companies need to know which part of the essential equipment will fail imminently so as to take action to prevent failure; financial institutions need to know which loan applications to approve/reject based on future ability to pay. In contrast, a project not driven by business needs is likely to be dropped when higher priorities arise in the future.

Netflix depended on its machine learning model to earn millions in revenue. The ability to predict well, even if imperfectly, has tremendous value. Netflix realized this early and adopted data-driven analytics with model predictions as a key corporate strategy.

These predictive models and machine learning applications are used in so many aspects of society that they define the modern way of doing business and living. Almost 80% of AI applications are in supervised learning.

3. Supervised Learning

Supervised machine learning is the clearest form of machine learning as the objective is prediction. Simply compare the prediction to actual data to get the prediction error. Thus, errors can be computed without ambiguity and improvements can be objectively measured. The historical actual values of the targeted variables serve as the "supervisor" in the data, telling the algorithm what is right/wrong and how much it is right/wrong.

We start by collecting a set of data that contains predictors (X variables) that could potentially predict the target outcome variable (Y variable). As an example, if someone is planning to buy an apartment in the market, the Y variable is the price of the apartment, X_1 is the size of the apartment, X_2 is the location, X_3 is the story of the apartment, X_4 is the distance to the nearest train station, etc. The dataset could be compiled from recent one-year apartment sale transactions. Then, we select a model that can learn to predict the Y variable using the X variables. Price is an example of a continuous Y variable.

In bank loan applications, X_1 is the size of the loan, X_2 is the income of the applicant, X_3 is the total debt of the applicant, X_4 is the credit score, etc. The Y variable is the categorical outcome variable — approval or rejection of the loan.

In credit card fraudulent transaction detection, X_1 is the amount of the transaction, X_2 is the location of the purchase, X_3 is the time of the purchase, etc. The Y variable is the categorical outcome variable — approving or blocking the transaction.

The most technical part is the choice and use of the selected model. There are numerous models. The most basic model is linear regression. Other models include ridge regression, lasso regression, multivariate adaptive regression splines, neural network, classification and regression tree (CART), random forest, and XGBoost.[3] The model is the mechanism whereby the AI learns to predict the

---

[3] For more detailed descriptions and explanations of the advanced models, please refer to Chew (Vol 1. 2021 and Vol. 2 forthcoming in 2025 est.).

Y variable using the X variables in the dataset. This process is also known as model training. The dataset given to the model to train it to predict the Y variable is known as the trainset. This training process ends when the model parameters are customized and optimized to the trainset, and the trainset error has been computed. Different models have different types and quantities of model parameters to optimize.

After selecting and training the model on the given dataset, we should test the model by computing the error on a testset. The testset could be a hold-out dataset from historical data or, if one can wait, a newly collected dataset in the near future. The error metrics of both the trainset and testset depend on the nature of the Y variable (continuous or categorical) and the desired properties of the prediction. The testset's error can then be used to identify the best model with the lowest error.

The supervised learning process can be viewed as follows:

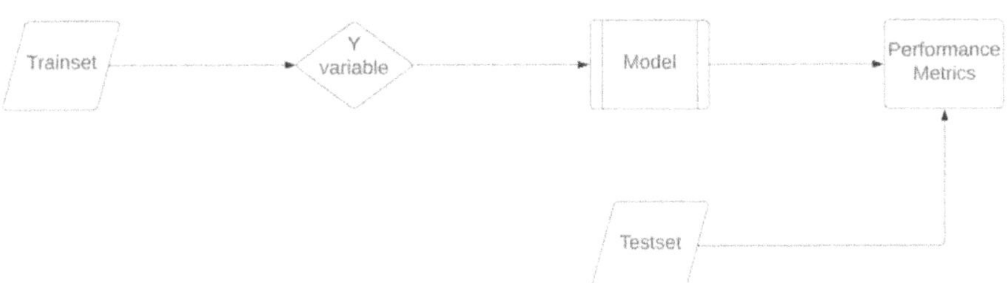

The model learns to predict the Y variable using the X variables in the trainset and then computes the chosen performance metrics. If the testset's performance is good enough, the model can be deployed in the business application.

4. Unsupervised Learning

In contrast to supervised learning, unsupervised learning is used if there is an absence of historical data about the target Y variable to guide the model training process. Hence, this approach is not meant to predict a specific target variable. We use unsupervised learning as a model-driven method to understand the data in a specific way. One can consider the dataset as comprising X variables only (no target Y variable).

Examples of unsupervised learning include clustering, principal component analysis, and association rules.

Clustering seeks to split the data into K groups, where members in the same group are alike. The value of K can be chosen based on business requirements/insights. Alternatively, statistical guidelines such as the elbow method may be used to determine a good value for K.

Principal component analysis is a way to reduce most of the information in the data to just a few variables. Those few variables (known as principal components) are linear combinations of all the X variables and are constructed based on variable importance ranking and correlation. Hence, one "reduces" the dimension of the problem. However, with modern machine learning models such as CART, random forest, or XGBoost that provide variable importance scoring, the attractiveness of the PCA method is reduced.

One popular unsupervised learning method is association rules, which serves to identify recommended rules based on combinations of events. Historically, it was created for cross-selling products in supermarkets, but has since been expanded to process non-retail transactions in domains such as medical diagnosis, workplace safety, and insurance claims analysis (see Lucas Lau and Arun Tripathi, 2001) by expanding the definition of "item." Association rules will generate a list of rules from the dataset by linking high-frequency events to one another and thus provide a statistical justification for a "recommendation." Hence, association rules is an unsupervised learning algorithm that can be used in recommendation systems on platforms such as Netflix, Amazon, Taobao, and Lazada.

Thus, unsupervised learning methods are more generic in their applications than supervised learning. Given that many business applications are very specific (e.g., approving loans, diagnosing disease, predicting default, estimating the length of stay, and forecasting prices), supervised learning applications are far more prevalent. The most attractive reason is that performance metrics are objective and well defined due to the presence of the Y variable in the dataset. In contrast, there is no Y variable in unsupervised learning.

5. Black-Box versus Glass-Box Machines

Given the central role played by model(s), a lot of emphasis is placed on the choice and optimization of the chosen model. There are models that are black boxes by nature and models that are glass boxes. In black-box models, it is hard to isolate the effect of each X variable on the Y variable. In glass-box models, it is easy to isolate effects and explain them to the audience. Neural networks[4] and deep learning are black-box models. In contrast, CART (Classification and Regression Tree)[5] is a glass-box model.

The importance of transparency will become evident if model predictions lead to a big loss for the company or deaths due to wrong treatment. A glass-box model is easily explainable, and the reasons for using this model in any unfortunate instance can be checked and found justified; however, the predictions from a black-box model are hard to explain in terms of X variables and difficult to comprehend.

On 30 November 2022, OpenAI launched ChatGPT — the single most important AI event in recent years. Suddenly, anyone could be a user of AI instead of only being subjected to AI predictions — your loan application is subjected to AI prediction of your credit risk, your waiting time at the emergency department is subjected to AI prediction of your injury or disease urgency, your insurance premium is subjected to AI prediction of a specific risk, etc. Since the invention of ChatGPT, the world's perception of AI changed remarkably, and new business models have been created. We can all use AI to be more efficient and productive in selected tasks, for free. ChatGPT requires two components: a large neural network (from machine learning) and a large amount of text

---

[4] Explained in Chew (2021), Chapter 9 and Rumelhart *et al.* (1986).
[5] Explained in Chew (2021), Chapter 8 and Breiman *et al.* (1983).

(from various text sources). The text processing capabilities of ChatGPT use concepts from text mining.

6. Text Mining

Many applications are based on structured data (numbers and categories) as applications (loan approvals, emergency room triage, insurance premiums, asset maintenance, ICU (Intensive Care Unit) monitoring, etc.) collect structured data from forms and/or sensors.

However, there are also applications for which insights can be extracted from text. Examples where text analysis can be applied include doctor's notes on a patient, feedback on new products, social media postings, news articles, and reports. The complication is that information is locked within words and words require interpretation and are often ambiguous without the context. It is far less straightforward for an algorithm to analyze text compared to numbers and categories.

If the quantity of text is small (for example, short comments in a survey form), then string processing might be sufficient. For big chunks of text (for example, speech, news articles, and reports), it will be more productive to use a text mining package to automate the analysis of words from sentences. One popular application of text mining is sentiment analysis, which seeks to identify the underlying sentiments in speeches, reports, news, etc. For detailed examples, refer to Chew (2021), Chapter 10.

7. ChatGPT and Generative AI

ChatGPT allows anyone to use AI easily. We are no longer just passively subjected to AI predictions (bank loans, patient treatment, customer marketing, etc.) but can actively use AI in our own area of work. One can use ChatGPT to write an article, draft emails, ask questions, get feedback, chat, etc. The ability to generate text automatically from just a few prompts is a useful generic capability. The source of data in ChatGPT comes from big collections of text (eBooks, selected websites) and then a neural network model to learn the sentences and context.

The data comprise the text. Hence, it is harder to analyze and interpret text than numbers as words are subjective and have different meanings, but are generally easier to collect (Wikipedia, forums, documents, etc.) and easier to use (emails, letters, documents, etc.).

A standard text mining process will break down the sequences of words into tokens. A massive neural network model with billions of parameters to be computed is then used to learn the connections between words and infer context. That is how ChatGPT is capable of constructing sentences by predicting the next word and generating different versions of textual outputs with the same input prompt.

The ability to learn from data in neural networks comes from calculating errors at each run of the model, assigning blame to each parameter, and most crucially, revising each parameter in the correct direction (either increasing or decreasing the parameter's value) to guarantee that each revision reduces overall error. This guarantee is crucial as it implies that, with sufficient computing power to complete sufficient runs of the model, the overall error is low enough to predict the next word with sufficient accuracy. The guarantee is achieved via backpropagation. This breakthrough is accomplished via an equation using the first derivative of the error function due to the parameters. The first derivative tells how the error will change via a small change in each parameter value (i.e., the tangent line interpretation of the first derivative) and hence allows the model to know how to change each of the parameters correctly, without human intervention. The choice of the error function (reasonable functions provided by default) and data allows the neural network model to learn to revise each parameter value automatically without human judgment.

A simple[6] neural network example provided in Chew (2021), Chapter 9, shows how to construct a single-layer neural network

---

[6] So that anyone can run a neural network on a laptop in seconds, without server or cloud computing resources.

(with 13 parameters) that predicts perfectly on a small set of data after 106 runs in less than one second. The neural network automatically learns from the error in each run and auto-revises each parameter value in each run.

ChatGPT is a new wave of AI that generates context. However, the underlying techniques are not new. Text mining and neural networks were established decades ago. What is new and useful is that they allow AI to be used by anyone, easily, to generate content that helps people in their everyday work.

In addition to text generation, one can also generate images, music, etc., by simply using images, music, videos, etc., as the source data instead of text. Sachin Tonk's chapter in this edited book volume provides more details on the use cases for generative AI.

8. Data as the Source of Strength in AI

The strength of AI comes from the underlying data. Regardless of structured (numbers and categories) or unstructured data (text, images, videos), one can collect more data and start making more data-driven decisions. In order to illustrate the use of data in supervised machine learning, we will briefly walk through the usefulness and value-add of a model that estimates apartment prices.

Example: Predicting housing prices based on house attributes.
Purchasing a home is the most important and substantial financial commitment for most citizens in developed nations. What are the variables that affect housing prices? The following is a proposed short list[7]:

- Location of the house,
- Size of the house,
- Story (or level) of the house,

---

[7] This is a short list, not an exhaustive list, and there are other factors not included.

- Train station within a few minutes' walk,
- Presence of amenities near the house,
- Condition of the house.

Most people understand the following:

- A centrally located house is more expensive, all else constant.
- The bigger the house, the more costly the housing price, all else constant.
- The higher the house, the more costly the housing price, all else constant.
- If a train station is within a short walking distance, the housing price is higher, all else constant.
- If there are amenities (supermarket, clinics, parks, etc.) within a short walking distance, the housing price is higher, all else constant.
- A well-maintained house is more expensive, all else constant.

But how do all the variables combine together to affect the housing price? What precisely is the premium value of a higher-floor housing unit compared to a lower floor? By training a model (linear regression, neural network, random forest, etc.) on historical housing sale transactions, the model can estimate and thus predict the price of a housing unit that considers all the variables in the dataset and quantitatively provide a numerical value for each attribute of the house. This is the usefulness and value-add of a model. Using a model on a dataset provides additional insights beyond just the raw data values and can answer "What-If" scenarios.

9. Data as the Source of Weakness in AI

Data can also be a source of weakness. The most common source of weakness is missing data or null data (also known as nonexistent data).

What is the estimated price of a flat that has an unblocked view of the South China Sea? If such cases are not in the dataset, they cannot be estimated directly by AI or machine learning. The data are missing but they exist, just not in your dataset.

In contrast, what is the estimated price of a flat that is 100 stories high? Such a flat (and hence data) does not exist as of 2024. Thus, it cannot be estimated directly by AI or machine learning.

This affects the way data professionals prepare the data. If data are missing (but exist), there are many ways to impute the missing data. For example, impute using the mean, median, or mode; estimate using linear regression, logistic regression, or random forest. If there are lots of missing data and these data cannot be collected in a reasonable time frame or within a reasonable cost, a popular solution is to use the classification and regression tree (CART) model to automatically handle all missing data values via the surrogate feature. This is the only model that can handle missing data automatically and in a principled manner without imputing the missing data values.[8]

The second common weakness is bias in the data. In a bank loan customer dataset, if all the loan applicants of race X are rejected by the credit department, and this dataset is used to train the machine learning model, the model will predict that all race X applicants are considered high risk and thus reject their loan applications. Even if there are good-risk race X applicants, the model will not approve the loan as such cases are not in the dataset. The human bank manager will need to be aware of biasness in the data and will have to manually review the loan application from race X when such a case surfaces.

Data are often only a tiny subset of reality. Relying on insufficient or biased data can lead to huge losses and even death.

10. Death from AI Wrong Predictions

In all applications (e.g., medical diagnosis and prognosis), no models are perfect. Even advanced AI models can be wrong sometimes.

---

[8] For details of surrogates in the CART model, refer to Chew (2021), Chapter 8.

But they can be useful and provide support to the medical experts. That's how the CART machine learning model (explained and dissected in Chew, 2001, Chapter 8) was invented, and it saved the lives of countless heart attack patients in the 1970s and 1980s. The CART model's accuracy is better than some ER doctors without blood test results but not perfect. This means some patients will be wrongly classified by CART. Fortunately, the model is just one component in the process and doctors are available on-site to monitor and correct mistakes.

However, tragedies from AI model predictions did occur. Several companies are in a race to develop the first self-driving car (without a human driver) ready for any road condition. In some cars-on-the-road trials, deaths occurred in part because the AI model was unable to distinguish the color of a vehicle from the color of the sky and environment.

Just as there are no perfect human experts, there is no perfect AI. Instead of blind trust in AI predictions, it is more useful to treat AI as another "expert" opinion and not a substitute for judgment and human decision-making.

References

Breiman, L., Friedman, J., Olshen, R. A., and Stone, C. J. (1983). *Classification and Regression Trees*. USA: Wadsworth.

Chew, C. H. (2021). *Artificial Intelligence, Analytics and Data Science. Volume 1: Core Concepts and Models*. Singapore: Cengage.

Lau, L. and Tripathi, A. (2001). Mine your business — A novel application of association rules for insurance claims analytics. *Casualty Actuarial Society E-Forum*, Winter 2011.

Rumelhart, D. E., Hinton, G. E., and Williams, R. J. (1986). Learning representations by back-propagating errors. *Nature*, 323(6088), 533–536.

Nick Street, W., Wolberg, W. H. and Mangasarian, O. L. "Nuclear feature extraction for breast tumor diagnosis", Proc. SPIE 1905, *Biomedical Image Processing and Biomedical Visualization*, (29 July 1993); https://doi.org/10.1117/12.148698

Chapter 10

Generative AI for Advanced Value Creation

Sachin Tonk

GovTech, Singapore
Sachin_TONK@tech.gov.sg

Abstract

Generative artificial intelligence (AI), a developing subfield within the domain of machine learning, has become a catalyst for profound transformation across many industries. Generative AI employs various machine learning techniques, including deep learning and probabilistic modeling, to represent and manipulate data distributions. This allows it to generate novel data points that fall within the learned distribution, effectively creating something new from what it has seen. This dynamic subset of AI is characterized by the exceptional capacity to synthesize novel data patterns from existing data, prompting a wave of innovation with wide-reaching implications. In this chapter, we will examine the state-of-the-art developments and multifaceted applications of generative AI, highlighting its key role in promoting value creation worth trillions of dollars in the digital landscape and its impact in the ongoing digital era. Generative AI also poses a unique set of challenges. This chapter will also analyze the hurdles faced by practitioners pertaining to data quality, model bias, and the imperatives for responsible AI deployment. Additionally, it will delve into the complex ethical concerns that surround generative AI and address questions about intellectual property, privacy concerns, and the potential for misuse. The evolution of generative AI has propelled creativity and problem-solving into uncharted territories for businesses and researchers. This chapter emphasizes generative AI's potential to drive invention, foster creativity, and intrinsically reshape the way we engage with data in the 21st century.

Keywords: Generative AI, deep learning, machine learning, neural networks, model bias, responsible AI, intellectual property, privacy concerns.

1. Introduction

First introduced as a subset of machine learning, Generative Artificial Intelligence (generative AI) has grown in recent years, reshaping value creation across diverse industries. According to the latest McKinsey report (McKinsey & Company, 2023) titled "The economic potential of generative AI," generative AI is predicted to add $2.6 trillion to $4.4 trillion annually. Approximately 75% of the potential value offered by generative AI applications can be attributed to four key domains: customer operations, marketing and sales, software engineering, and research and development.

Generative AI is fundamentally restructuring the operational underpinnings of various industries worldwide, with a particular focus on banking, life sciences, and the tech sector. The field holds the promise of reshaping the nature of work by enhancing the skills of individual workers through the automation of specific tasks that make up 60–70% of the employee's time. Generative AI has already significantly boosted labor productivity across various sectors such as content creation and marketing, design and manufacturing, healthcare and research, and administrative and customer service.

Generative AI represents a shift, creating new data from existing information. Recent progress, fueled by advancements in neural networks and deep learning, transcends sectors like healthcare, finance, and manufacturing. This transformative impact enhances operational efficiency and yields innovative solutions. The essence of generative AI lies in its unique ability to infuse data with vitality, going beyond analysis to create and design. It contributes to diverse outcomes, from synthetic medical imagery and optimized financial models to creative content generation and improved manufacturing precision.

2. Understanding Generative AI

Generative AI leads artificial intelligence, focusing on creating novel data from existing information. This ability relies on implementing algorithms and models, with each contributing to the generative process. Important aspects of generative AI include neural networks, deep learning, and a variety of generative models, all of which form the foundational pillars of this innovative field (Yann LeCun, 2015).

Neural networks, central to generative AI, function as key components in pattern recognition, data generation, and information enhancement (Schmidhuber, 2015). Their adaptability makes them indispensable tools in the creation of value through generative AI, allowing for the unveiling of hidden data structures and the development of previously overlooked information. This catalyzes transformative advancements in sectors like healthcare, finance, and creative industries (Yann LeCun, 2015).

Within the realm of generative models, several foundational concepts have paved the way for the expansive developments within generative AI:

1. Generative Adversarial Networks (GANs), initially presented by Goodfellow and colleagues in 2014 (Goodfellow, 2014), have ushered in a significant transformation in the realm of generative AI. GANs work on a unique adversarial principle, wherein a generator and a discriminator immerse in an ongoing contest. The generator's objective is to produce increasingly realistic data, while the discriminator's role is to distinguish between real and generated data. This adversarial interplay impacts the creation of data that are often practically indiscernible from accurate data, granting GANs significant utility in an assortment of applications, particularly in fields such as image synthesis and data augmentation. GANs

are located within the broader framework of machine learning, drawing inspiration from the work of Ian Goodfellow and his colleagues, and employing loss functions reminiscent of noise contrastive estimation (Grnarova *et al.*, 2019). The practical application of GANs gained significant momentum in 2017, initially focusing on enhancing the quality of images, particularly in the context of generating lifelike human faces.

The roots of adversarial networks can be traced back to Olli Niemitalo's blog post in 2010, a concept closely related to Conditional GANs. In the context of a relentless examination of the conversion of 2D images to 3D, the method begins with the acquisition of pertinent datasets and the establishment of benchmarks using key features, as discussed by Wu, Zhang, Xue, Freeman, and Tenenbaum in 2016 (Jiajun Wu, 2016). This includes the stages of live data collection, threshold calculation, and suitability scoring. Subsequent phases encompass image merging and preprocessing, which involves segmentation and cleansing, followed by GAN training. The intended outcomes of this process revolve around pattern analysis and the precision of image generation.

2. Variational Autoencoders (VAEs), pioneered by Kingma and Welling in 2013 (Kingma, 2013), offer a probabilistic path to generative modeling. Unlike cleanly discriminative methods and traditional generative models, VAEs concentrate on encoding data into a lower-dimensional latent space, allowing manipulation before decoding them back into the original data distribution. This method improves the discourse on generative and discriminative models by showcasing a process that amalgamates the strengths of both paradigms. VAEs find functional utility in diverse domains, including data compression, denoising, and the generation of novel data points. They can clean up messy images, generate missing parts of songs, or even invent fresh designs based on existing styles. In short, VAEs unlock the door to creative data manipulation and generation across various fields, from medicine to music to manufacturing.

Similarly, as highlighted by Banerjee (2007), generative models, while usually efficient, tend to create more powerful assumptions about the data, possibly showing improved bias when the model's assumptions do not align with the data distribution.

3. Recurrent Neural Networks (RNNs), presented by Hochreiter and Schmidhuber in 1997 (Hochreiter, 1997), stand as a powerful category of neural networks, ideally served for processing sequential data, including domains such as time series analysis and natural language processing. These networks maintain a memory component that stimulates them to capture temporal dependencies and generate sequences of data, making them indispensable in applications like language modeling and speech synthesis.

RNNs mark a considerable improvement in the domain of neural networks, offering an express benefit through their internal memory. Notably, RNNs exhibit promise when handling sequential data, encompassing areas such as speech, text, financial data, audio, video, weather, and various other domains. This internal memory capability gives RNNs a deeper understanding of sequences and their contextual importance, setting them apart from alternative algorithms.

These foundational generative models have laid the bedrock for the vast abilities of generative AI, where the domains of learning and creativity converge to pioneer new borders in data generation and information enhancement. The combination of GANs and VAEs allows for the creation of realistic and diverse data samples. The inclusion of RNNs enables generative AI to understand and generate sequential data, enhancing its capabilities in tasks like text generation or video synthesis. The integration of GANs and VAEs facilitates the exploration of a meaningful latent space, providing control over the generated output.

3. Latest Developments in Generative AI

Generative AI models like GPT and DALL-E have benefited from advancements in earlier generative AI models. GANs and VAEs enhance realism and diversity. RNN principles influence GPT for sequential data. Transfer learning and pre-training in GPT capture context. DALL-E combines GANs and transformers for multimodal learning. Latent space exploration, improved training, and iterative refinement techniques contribute to enhanced capabilities in both models.

GPT-3 (Brown, 2020), designed by OpenAI, marks a climactic point in the development of generative AI. This language model has displayed exceptional versatility, excelling in a wide range of tasks. GPT-3's proficiencies encircle text generation, language translation, content summarization, and even natural language understanding. It has rapidly taken a central role in industries where language processing is essential, including applications in chatbots, content creation, and automated customer support.

DALL-E (Radford, 2021), another groundbreaking product by OpenAI, tackles the domain of image generation, virtually breaking down the conventional barriers between textual definitions and visual content. DALL-E can deliver images based on textual inputs, rendering it a powerful tool for creative professionals and designers. This model has sparked the creativity of artists and innovators by converting written descriptions into visually stunning artworks.

CLIP (Ramesh, 2021), a cooperative project conducted by OpenAI and Microsoft Research, redefines the connection between images and text. By granting AI systems the capability to understand both images and text at the same time, CLIP presents untried applications in image classification, content retrieval, and contextual understanding. This groundbreaking model contains the potential to revolutionize the way we confront visual and textual data, virtually bridging the longstanding distance between these two distinct forms of information.

These state-of-the-art models, symbolizing merely a fraction of the wider landscape of generative AI innovations, have left an unforgettable mark throughout a multitude of industries. From healthcare to entertainment, they have shown new paradigms for data generation and content creation, unlocking priceless insights and encouraging originality on an unparalleled scale. The deployment of these models is reshaping how we approach various tasks, steering innovation and automation that once seemed beyond reach.

The utility of these generative models expands further than their original design, functioning as triggers for creative inventiveness and further improvement in artificial intelligence. Their potential is not restricted by the initial purposes of their creators but instead develops as researchers and practitioners recognize unexplored applications and harness their abilities to tackle a myriad of challenges.

4. Applications of Innovative Generative AI

Generative AI, with its transformative abilities, is revolutionizing diverse industries by delivering innovative answers that not only increase efficiency but also open up new boundaries for progress. It has been demonstrated to be a versatile and vital tool throughout a spectrum of domains.

4.1. *Healthcare*

Generative AI is taking a climactic role in healthcare, compelling breakthroughs in diagnostic image generation, drug discovery, and the evolution of personalized medicine plans. For example, it excels in synthesizing artificial medical images, such as X-rays, MRIs, and CT scans, which can supplement limited datasets and remarkably improve the precision of disease detection (Shin, 2016). Furthermore, in the area of drug discovery, generative AI expedites the designation of potential drug candidates by developing molecular structures with desired properties (Gómez-Bombarelli, 2018). This is particularly essential in the context of emerging diseases and the critical demand for accelerated drug development.

4.2. *Finance*

Generative AI is directing a significant change in the financial sector. It plays a key part in algorithmic trading, risk assessment, and fraud detection. In algorithmic trading, generative AI examines historical market data and develops more effective trading strategies. Furthermore, it improves risk assessment by leveraging its predictive abilities to predict credit default events via the breakdown of financial data (Gernmanno, 2019). Besides, generative AI proves invaluable in the evolution of fraud detection systems, as it can generate synthetic data that mimic various fraud scenarios for better-preparing anomaly detection algorithms.

4.3. *Entertainment*

The entertainment industry has harnessed the visionary potential of generative AI, ushering a revolution in content creation, virtual actors, and video game design. AI models like DALL-E are instrumental in developing diverse creative content, spanning art, music, and literature, thereby expanding the horizons of artistic expression. Virtual actors, trained in speech, gestures, and facial expressions, are increasingly incorporated into various media formats (Ginosar, 2019). Likewise, the design of video games is becoming increasingly automated, with generative AI crafting game environments, characters, and quests (Summerville *et al.*, 2016).

4.4. *Manufacturing*

Generative AI is empowering manufacturers to improve product design, production processes, and predictive maintenance. It assists in product design by developing 3D models and prototypes, promoting innovative product development (Rossit *et al.*, 2019). For optimization, generative AI constructs designs that are not only efficient but also tailored to precise requirements (Li *et al.*, 2021). Unlike traditional simulation, GAI is not limited to predefined scenarios and manually crafted models. It offers advantages in handling complex systems, incomplete data, and personalized maintenance. Predictive maintenance systems depend on generative models to simulate equipment behavior and forecast maintenance needs, guaranteeing seamless operations.

Generative AI facilitates and improves manufacturing processes, allowing businesses to design superior products and handle their equipment with precision. The integration of generative AI into these industries is encouraging a profound change, redefining the potential and efficiency in healthcare, finance, entertainment, and manufacturing. This technology is catalyzing new paradigms, resulting in more useful diagnostic tools, ingenious financial strategies, creative expression, and state-of-the-art manufacturing methods.

5. Techniques for Innovative Generative AI

The extraordinary success of generative AI in compelling value creation is embedded in a diverse set of techniques, each developed to improve the abilities of AI systems.

Transfer Learning (Malte and Ratadiya, 2019): Paramount to generative AI's adaptability is the process of transfer learning. This technique allows models to leverage preexisting details from one domain and apply them properly in another, lessening the reliance on comprehensive labeled datasets. Models originally trained in one domain can be fine-tuned for particular tasks or adjusted to wholly new domains, making generative AI deployment more accessible and cost-effective.

For instance, transfer learning in fashion design has transformed the industry. It takes pre-trained models, and masters of style, and fine-tunes them to specific brands, trends, or even individual preferences. So, you get personalized recommendations, on-demand trend-inspired designs, and realistic virtual try-on experiences. This AI magic translates to reduced costs, happier customers, and smarter inventory management for fashion houses of all sizes. Also, pre-trained large language models are becoming increasingly ubiquitous across different industries.

Reinforcement Learning (Sutton and Barto, 1998): Reinforcement learning, inspired by behavioral psychology, trains AI systems with the capability to understand and acclimate through a cycle of trial and error. This approach is especially useful in generative AI, particularly in content creation. AI models can test and refine their outcomes based on feedback from humans, metrics, or internal evaluations, allowing them to generate diverse, context-aware, and adaptive content.

Unsupervised Learning: Unsupervised learning is a foundational technique that plays a key role in generative AI. It allows AI systems to uncover hidden patterns and systems in data without depending on labeled examples. This versatility makes unsupervised learning specifically valuable in applications where the expected output is not predefined, such as creative content generation. In generative AI, unsupervised learning operates like an artist exploring a blank canvas. It delves into unlabeled data, seeking hidden patterns and structures without being told what to look for. This freedom makes it perfect for creative content generation, where the goal is not to replicate something specific but to unleash novel possibilities.

Data Augmentation (Shorten and Khoshgoftaar, 2019): Data augmentation is instrumental in boosting the diversity and robustness of data utilized by generative AI. This technique presents controlled variations and perturbations to the existing dataset, ensuring that AI models can generate suitable and noteworthy content while managing a myriad of scenarios and data inputs. Data augmentation is instrumental when there are limited and imbalanced datasets available. AWS SageMaker, Google AI Platform, and Azure Machine Learning offer data augmentation pre-processing options along with specialized libraries such as imgaug (images), nlpaug (text), and torchaudio (audio).

Domain Adaptation: Motivated by transfer learning, domain adaptation empowers generative AI to adjust its learning to varying environments and contexts. This is notably advantageous when deploying AI systems in various real-world scenarios, ensuring that they stay effective and relevant in diverse contexts.

Real-world case studies underscore the palpable impact of these techniques in different domains. For example, in healthcare, transfer learning has revolutionized medical image analysis. Pre-trained models, originally designed for natural language processing tasks, have been adjusted for image analysis tasks, decreasing the necessity for expansive labeled datasets (Esteva *et al.*, 2019). This innovation has enormously improved the efficiency and accuracy of disease detection in healthcare applications.

6. Challenges and Ethical Considerations

Generative AI, while holding tremendous promise, also presents a range of challenges and ethical concerns that merit exhaustive analysis and proactive surveillance:

- *Bias in AI-generated content* (Obermeyer *et al.*, 2019): A major challenge lies in the existence of bias in AI-generated content. The learning process of AI models, guided by extensive datasets, can inadvertently perpetuate the biases ingrained in their training data. This can lead to the generation of biased outcomes that strengthen stereotypes and discrimination. Managing and mitigating bias in generative AI is a multifaceted challenge, necessitating not only thorough curation of training data but also the growth of models that are continuously monitored and audited to eliminate these intrinsic biases.

- *Data privacy* (Martínez *et al.*, 2023): Generative AI models, particularly those trained on sensitive and personal data, present significant considerations concerning data privacy. The very act of developing content can inadvertently lead to the exposure of private information. To mitigate these privacy risks, the evolution and implementation of advanced privacy-preserving techniques, alongside robust security measures, are critical. Protecting personal details and privacy in generative AI applications requires active responsibility.

- *Security against adversarial attacks* (Akhtar and Mian, 2018): The susceptibility of generative AI systems to malicious attacks is another urgent concern. Adversaries can exploit AI-generated content, employing it to mislead or harm individuals and organizations. To guarantee the dependability and security of generative AI applications, it is vital to design robust security measures. These efforts must contain not only the technological fortification of AI models but also the organization of protocols for the early detection and alleviation of adversarial threats.

- *Ethical considerations*: Ethical considerations for the deployment of generative AI span across multiple domains. As generative AI systems evolve to become increasingly pervasive, questions covering their influence on society, culture, and human values appear as prominent concerns. The accountable and safe deployment of generative AI necessitates the expansion of thorough ethical policies and regulatory frameworks. These policies should not only encourage the ethical use of

AI-generated content but also handle the more expansive importance of human values and societal well-being.

In handling these multifaceted challenges and ethical concerns, the development, deployment, and continued monitoring of generative AI stand as complicated yet crucial endeavors. The capacities of this technology must be harnessed in a way that promotes societal well-being while reducing possible risks and ensuring the reliable use of AI-generated content.

7. Future Trends in Generative AI

Generative AI is on the cusp of significant breakthroughs, with emerging applications and evolving challenges shaping its future. As it continues to develop, generative AI is expected to integrate seamlessly with other advanced technologies, driving innovation and unlocking new opportunities for value creation.

Integration with blockchain (Swan, 2015): A fascinating opportunity on the horizon is the combination of generative AI and blockchain technology. Blockchain, known for its qualities of security and transparency, presents a vigorous platform for tasks like AI-generated content verification, intellectual property protection, and content ownership tracking. This intersection vows to open innovative avenues for safe and transparent content creation and distribution.

Leveraging quantum computing (Preskill, 2018): Quantum computing, with its exceptional computational power, can reshape generative AI. Quantum algorithms can seriously expedite complex generative tasks, allowing swifter and additional sophisticated content generation. The synergy between generative AI and quantum computing is poised to deliver breakthroughs in areas such as scientific research, cryptography, and creative content generation.

Multimodal content generation: One of the imminent breakthroughs in the realm of generative AI is the evolution of even more advanced models capable of comprehending and generating content across diverse modalities, including text, images, and audio. This evolution will empower generative AI systems to create content that seamlessly blends various forms of media, resulting in more genuine and coherent content generation. The importance of this advancement extends across a wide array of sectors, encircling domains like entertainment, marketing, and education.

Democratization of generative AI: Generative AI is anticipated to become more accessible to a broader range of users, such as content creators, businesses, and individuals. As user-friendly tools and outlets are developed, generative AI may be democratized, facilitating people to harness their creativity with the assistance of AI. This democratization can encourage an increase in content and creative expressions, further developing industries and communities.

Ethical and regulatory focus: The challenges revolving around data security are expected to multiply in the future. To address these issues, stricter policies and ethical regulations must be established to guarantee responsible AI use. Regulatory bodies and industry stakeholders would have to play an active role in managing and enforcing these policies. These restrictions are vital for upholding fairness, responsibility, and clarity in AI-generated content.

The future of generative AI is characterized by invention, synergy with other cutting-edge technologies, and a dedication to reliable and ethical AI deployment. It holds the capacity to revolutionize content creation, enhance accessibility, and ensure that generative AI persists to help humanity while managing its growing challenges.

8. Conclusion

Generative AI stands as a formidable driving force behind advanced value creation across a spectrum of industries in the contemporary world. The latest developments and innovative applications of generative AI vividly illustrate its transformative potential. Yet, as this field continues to evolve and mature, it becomes increasingly apparent that its multifaceted landscape demands in-depth consideration of ethical dimensions and the anticipation of future trends to harness its full potential.

The influence of generative AI is indisputable. It has guided technology in a new era of creativity, efficiency, and innovation. Models like GPT-3, DALL-E, and CLIP have proven the remarkable variety of capabilities that generative AI brings to the table. From healthcare to finance, entertainment to manufacturing, generative AI is reshaping the way we approach problems, enabling novel solutions, and enhancing our ability to create value.

The ethical concerns surrounding generative AI are as essential as its potential. As we delve into the creative domains of AI-generated content, there are still issues of bias, privacy concerns, and adversarial threats. Bias in AI-generated content is not only an issue of algorithms; it is a review of the biases present in the training data and society at large. Privacy, an indispensable human right, becomes increasingly elaborate as generative AI's abilities develop, pitching questions about data ownership and consent.

Nevertheless, even within these challenges lie possibilities. The expectation of emerging trends, such as the integration of generative AI with blockchain and quantum computing, is a testament to the technology's ability to adjust and flourish. Blockchain's transparent and secure ledger system can bring about a new era of confidence in AI-generated content, guaranteeing proper attribution, privilege, and protection of intellectual property. The computational power of quantum computing, merged with generative AI, may open new dimensions in creativity, research, and cryptography.

The expansion of multimodal content generation vows more immersive and cohesive content. In the future, generative AI systems may be adept at seamlessly combining text, images, and audio, thereby redefining the opportunities in entertainment, marketing, and education.

Furthermore, the democratization of generative AI will allow a wider variety of users to partake in creative content generation. This accessibility will not only encourage innovation but also democratize the tools of ideation, facilitating a more inclusive and eclectic creative landscape.

As generative AI progresses, it is incumbent upon the technical community, regulatory bodies, and society as a whole to manage the ethical dimensions. More rigorous approaches and ethical frameworks will be fundamental to make sure that generative AI serves society responsibly and equitably.

In conclusion, generative AI has proved to be a transformative force, driving state-of-the-art value creation. Its potential knows no bounds, and its favorable influence on industries and society is already profound. The journey onward requires a congruous approach, recognizing both the opportunities and the obligations. Generative AI has the capacity to transform the way we develop, communicate, and innovate. It is up to us to direct its development along a path that helps all of humanity.

References

Akhtar, Z. and Mian, A. (2018). Threat of adversarial attacks on deep learning in computer vision: A survey. *IEEE Access* 6, 14410–14430.

Banerjee, A. (2007). An analysis of logistic models: Exponential family connections and online performance. In: *Proceedings of the 2007 SIAM International Conference on Data Mining*. SIAM, pp. 204–215.

Brown, T. B., *et al.* (2020). Language models are few-shot learners. In Advances in Neural Information Processing Systems (pp. 1877–1901).

Esteva, A., *et al.* (2019). A guide to deep learning in healthcare. *Nature Medicine* 25(1), 24–29.

Gernmanno, T., et al. (2019). "Machine learning and decision support system on credit scoring." Neural Computing and Applications, 2019, 14, pp. 9809-9826.

Ginosar, S., et al. (2019). Everybody Dance Now. In Proceedings of the IEEE/CVF International Conference on Computer Vision (ICCV) 2019.

Gómez-Bombarelli, R., et al. (2018). Automatic chemical design using a data-driven continuous representation of molecules. ACS Central Science, 4(2), 268-276.

Goodfellow, I., Pouget-Abadie, J., Mirza, M., Xu, B., Warde-Farley, D., Ozair, S., ... and Bengio, Y. (2014). Generative adversarial nets. In: *Advances in Neural Information Processing Systems*, pp. 2672–2680.

Grnarova, P., Beery, S., Hadfield, R., Boyd, D., and Sheperd, D. (2019). Noise contrastive estimation and loss function used in present GAN. *arXiv preprint* arXiv:1905.05801.

Hochreiter, S., & Schmidhuber, J. (1997). Long short-term memory. Neural Computation, 9(8), 1735–1780.

Kingma, D. P., & Welling, M. (2013). Auto-encoding variational bayes. In Proceedings of the International Conference on Learning Representations (ICLR).

LeCun, Y., *et al.* (2015). Deep learning. Nature, 521(7553), 436–444.

Li, N., *et al.* (2021). Remaining useful life prediction based on a multi-sensor data fusion model. *IEEE Transactions on Industrial Electronics* 69(10), 7053–7062.

Malte, A. and Ratadiya, P. (2019). Evolution of transfer learning in natural language processing. *arXiv preprint* arXiv:1910.07370.

Martínez, G., *et al.* (2023). Towards understanding the interplay of generative artificial intelligence and the internet.

McKinsey & Company. (2023). The economic potential of generative AI: The next productivity frontier.

Obermeyer, Z., *et al.* (2019). Dissecting racial bias in an algorithm used to manage the health of populations. *Science* 366(6464), 447–453.

Preskill, J. (2018). Quantum computing in the NISQ era and beyond. *Quantum* 2, 79.

Radford, A., *et al.* (2021). Learning Transferable Visual Models From Natural Language Supervision. In Proceedings of the International Conference on Machine Learning (ICML) (pp. 8748–8763).

Ramesh, A., *et al.* (2021). DALL·E: Creating Images from Text. OpenAI.

Rossit, D., *et al.* (2019). A data-driven scheduling approach to smart manufacturing. *Journal of Industrial Information Integration* 15, 69–79.

Schmidhuber, J. (2015). Deep learning in neural networks: An overview. *Neural Networks* 61, 85–117.

Shin, H., *et al.* (2016). Deep convolutional neural networks for computer-aided detection: CNN architectures, dataset characteristics, and transfer learning. IEEE Transactions on Medical Imaging, 35(5), 1285–1298.

Shorten, C. and Khoshgoftaar, T. M. (2019). A survey on image data augmentation for deep learning. *Journal of Big Data* 6(1), 1–48.

Summerville, A. J., *et al.* (2016). Procedural content generation via machine learning (PCGML). In: *Proceedings of the International Conference on Computational Creativity*, pp. 62–69.

Sutton, R. S. & Barto, A. G. (1998). Reinforcement Learning: An Introduction. Cambridge, MA: MIT Press.

Swan, M. (2015). Blockchain: A Blueprint for a New Economy. Sebastopol, CA: O'Reilly Media.

Wu, J., *et al.* (2016). Multimodal generative models for 3D shape generation. In Proceedings of the IEEE Conference on Computer Vision and Pattern Recognition (pp. 143–152).

Chapter 11

Tipping the Scales with AI: Harnessing Data and AI to Enhance Business Value

Michael Taylor

Siemens Mobility Digital Services, Singapore
taylormichael@siemens.com

Abstract

As more organizations seek to leverage the power of artificial intelligence (AI) to create new efficiencies and a sustainable competitive advantage, data leaders are increasingly spearheading transformational programs. But what is needed to launch an AI project? Can AI outcomes be trusted? What are the main ways in which AI can fail? How can those failures be avoided? What new tools and techniques can help business leaders turbocharge and operationalize their data and AI programs? We will share some best practices, learned from successful machine learning projects at industry-leading clients, that can help data leaders think about AI and data, democratize these capabilities, strengthen the data-to-insight-to-action loop, and realize stronger results.

Keywords: Artificial intelligence, digital transformation, predictive maintenance, condition monitoring, data quality, value creation.

1. Introduction

In the dynamic tapestry of today's global marketplace, businesses are facing both challenges and opportunities of monumental proportions. This dual-faced phenomenon is a direct consequence of the ever-expanding realm of digital information and the emergent capabilities of artificial intelligence (AI). As streams of data flow like rivers into vast oceans of information, AI stands at the helm, guiding businesses through uncharted territories, unveiling treasures of insights.

Gone are the days when businesses solely relied on tangible assets like brick-and-mortar infrastructure, machinery, or inventory to steer their growth. The modern business landscape, rich with digital footprints, demands a new kind of prowess — the ability to extract meaning from a deluge of data. This shift has not just created new paradigms for existing industries but has also given birth to entirely new sectors and innovative frontiers.

With every digital interaction, from a simple online purchase to complex supply chain logistics, data are generated. These data, vast and varied, have the latent power to provide granular insights, forecast trends, and inform strategies. However, the sheer volume can be overwhelming. This is where AI takes center stage. AI, with its analytical might, possesses the capability to sift through the data, identifying patterns and making connections that the human mind might overlook.

So, what does this transformative synergy between data and AI signify for businesses? It represents a game-changing advantage for those ready to embrace it. By effectively leveraging AI, businesses can transcend traditional barriers, innovate at breakneck speeds, and most importantly offer unprecedented value to their stakeholders.

But the journey to harnessing this synergy is neither straightforward nor without its unique set of challenges. How have pioneering enterprises navigated these waters to turn potential into prosperity? What pitfalls have they encountered, and what triumphs have they celebrated? This chapter embarks on a deep dive into these questions, aiming to illuminate the pathways of AI-driven value creation. By its conclusion, you will not only have a holistic understanding of the transformative impact of AI on businesses but also actionable insights to chart your own course in this brave new world.

2. The Rise of Data as the New Oil

The phrase "Data is the new oil" has echoed throughout the corridors of modern industry for years now. While at first glance the comparison might seem abstract — one being a tangible resource, the other a digital entity — the parallels drawn are profound. Just as oil powered the industrial revolutions of the past, acting as the lifeblood of innovations and economies, data are now driving the digital revolution, shaping the contours of businesses and societies at large.

In the conclusion of our introduction, we hinted at the transformative synergy between data and AI. But before we delve deeper into how AI is the alchemical force that transforms this "digital oil" into gold, it is crucial to understand the ascent of data itself.

- **From obscurity to ubiquity:** Not too long ago, data were an afterthought for many businesses, often considered a byproduct of operations rather than a central asset. However, the shift from analog to digital, spurred by the internet and subsequent technological advancements, changed everything. Suddenly, every transaction, interaction, and even inaction began producing data.
- **The data deluge:** Today, we are inundated with data. Every click, swipe, like, share, and tweet contributes to an ever-growing digital repository. From sensors in smart cities measuring traffic patterns to wearable devices monitoring our heart rates, data generation is ceaseless. This proliferation is not just quantitative but also qualitative, with data types diversifying into structured, unstructured, and semi-structured formats.

- **The economic impact of data:** Much like oil, the value rarely comes from raw data but from data in their refined form. When processed and analyzed, data fuel business strategies, inform decisions, and spawn entirely new business models. Companies that recognized this early on, like Amazon, Google, and Facebook, are now titans of the tech industry, having built empires by adeptly mining, refining, and monetizing their data reservoirs.
- **Interdependence with AI:** With great volume comes great complexity. The human capability to analyze data has its limits, especially when confronted with the vast seas of data available today. This is where AI enters the narrative. AI, with its ability to parse, learn from, and act upon data at scales beyond human comprehension, has become the indispensable refinery for this new oil. This interdependence between data as a resource and AI as a tool to extract value underscores the central theme of our exploration.

By establishing data as the lifeblood of the digital age, businesses are positioned at a pivotal moment in history. The subsequent sections will shed light on the mechanisms, strategies, and technologies that allow businesses to harness this resource, turning potential into tangible value.

3. Fundamentals of AI in Business

In the contemporary digital landscape where data reign supreme, artificial intelligence (AI) stands as their most loyal and potent vassal. Building on our understanding of data's unparalleled significance, it becomes pivotal to delve into the machinery that can translate this data deluge into actionable business insights.

Artificial Intelligence, at its core, simulates human intelligence processes in machines. It embodies the capability of machines to learn, reason, and self-correct. An essential facet of AI is machine learning (ML), where systems are not explicitly programmed but taught to refine their algorithms based on data. This capacity for iterative learning from data makes ML an invaluable asset for businesses seeking to derive meaning from vast datasets.

Taking the complexity a notch higher is deep learning. Here, inspired by the human brain structure, neural networks process data in layered architectures, enabling breakthroughs in fields like image and speech recognition.

Revisiting our earlier analogy, if data are likened to the new oil, then AI emerges as the advanced refining mechanism. Raw oil, without refining, remains less valuable. In the same vein, without AI, the extensive data repositories businesses amass would stay indecipherable and underutilized. This symbiotic relationship between data and AI is the linchpin redefining competitive advantage, urging businesses to deepen their understanding and integration of AI.

As we advance in our exploration, it becomes unmistakably clear that the melding of data and AI represents not merely a trend but a seismic shift in business paradigms. The onus now lies on businesses to harness this convergence, translating potential into unparalleled value.

4. Strategies for Effective Data Harnessing

In the dance of digital transformation, while data provide the rhythm and AI the moves, it is the strategic choreography that ensures a harmonious performance. Recognizing the value of data and the capability of AI is only the beginning; businesses must also craft effective strategies to tap into this potential seamlessly.

The journey of data from their generation to utilization in AI-driven decision-making is intricate. Every byte of data captured holds the promise of insights, but only if harnessed correctly. The following are the essential elements to consider:

- **Holistic data ecosystems:** Crafting a comprehensive data ecosystem is foundational. This entails creating environments where data from diverse sources are integrated, cleansed, and readied for analysis. Such ecosystems, when maintained, ensure a steady and reliable flow of quality data to fuel AI algorithms.

- **Prioritizing data privacy:** In an age where data breaches and privacy concerns make headlines, businesses must prioritize data protection. Beyond legal compliance, this demonstrates a commitment to stakeholders and builds trust — a currency as valuable as the data itself.
- **Investing in talent and training:** Harnessing data is not solely about technology. Human expertise, particularly those skilled in data science and AI, is vital. Additionally, training the broader workforce to be data-literate fosters a culture where data-driven decision-making becomes second nature.
- **Agile and scalable architectures:** The volume and variety of data available are constantly expanding. Businesses must adopt agile architectures that not only handle current data loads but can also scale effortlessly with future demands.
- **Actionable insights over data hoarding:** While the allure of collecting vast amounts of data is strong, the focus should always be on quality over quantity. Data that do not provide actionable insights can become a liability, consuming storage and processing resources.

In the railway industry, for example (based on my experience with many of our mobility clients), the strategic integration of data and AI serves as a prime example of effective digital transformation. A comprehensive data ecosystem is established, integrating diverse data sources such as train operations, passenger information, weather updates, and maintenance records. These integrated data are meticulously cleansed and prepared for analysis, ensuring their reliability and accuracy. Prioritizing data privacy is also crucial; the railway system employs robust security measures to protect sensitive passenger and operational data, thus maintaining compliance with regulations and ensuring passenger trust.

Key to harnessing the data effectively is the company's investment in both technology and people. Specialized talent in data science and AI is brought on board to manage and interpret the complex data ecosystem. Simultaneously, existing employees undergo training to enhance their data literacy, enabling them to make informed decisions based on AI insights. The data infrastructure itself is designed to be agile and scalable, capable of accommodating future data expansion as the network grows or adopts new sensor technologies.

Rather than merely collecting data, the railway system focuses on extracting actionable insights. AI algorithms are employed to analyze operational data for predictive maintenance, optimize travel schedules using passenger data, and enhance safety measures by evaluating real-time weather conditions. These actionable insights result in tangible improvements like reduced downtimes, enhanced passenger experience, and increased safety. Through this holistic approach to data management and AI integration, the railway industry exemplifies the transformation of a traditional transport network into a data-driven, AI-enhanced enterprise, showcasing the power and potential of digital innovation in a complex industry.

5. Mastering the Convergence

As enterprises embark on integrating AI and human expertise, a deeper understanding of this convergence becomes essential. Pioneering organizations have illustrated how this synergy can be effectively achieved. These companies have strategically invested in AI technologies, ensuring they are finely tuned to their operational needs. They have also placed significant emphasis on upskilling their workforce, recognizing the crucial role of human collaboration with AI in maximizing data potential. This holistic approach extends beyond technological investment to fostering a collaborative, innovative culture and adopting ethical and compliant AI practices. By embracing an iterative implementation strategy and focusing on customer-centric AI applications, these enterprises have successfully navigated the complexities of AI and human synergy. Their journey underscores the importance of not just collecting data but also leveraging it through strategic AI integration, turning potential challenges into pathways for innovation and business success.

Connecting these strategies with our earlier discussions, it is evident that data's potential is akin to a locked treasure chest. AI represents the key, but without the right strategies — the map to this treasure — businesses may find themselves lost in the vastness of the digital sea. Embracing effective data-harnessing techniques ensures that companies can navigate these waters with precision, turning potential pitfalls into prosperous ventures.

6. Optimizing the Data-to-Insight-to-Action Cycle in Modern Businesses

In the evolving landscape of digital business, optimizing the data-to-insight-to-action cycle is pivotal for any company looking to leverage AI effectively. This cycle is a continuous process where data are not only collected and analyzed but also actively used to drive strategic decisions and actions.

1. **Data collection and integration:**
   - The cycle begins with robust data collection. Businesses must gather diverse datasets, ranging from customer interactions to operational metrics to market trends.
   - Effective integration of the data is crucial. Disparate data sources should be consolidated into a cohesive system, ensuring data compatibility and consistency.
2. **Insight generation:**
   - The heart of the cycle lies in transforming integrated data into meaningful insights. This involves deploying advanced analytics and AI models tailored to the specific needs of the business.
   - Generating actionable insights requires the AI to not only be accurate but also contextually relevant, providing clarity on customer behavior, market dynamics, or operational efficiencies.

3. **Actionable intelligence:**
   - The crux of the cycle is converting insights into concrete actions. For instance, market analysis insights might inform product development, while customer behavior insights could shape marketing strategies.
   - Establishing a feedback loop is essential. The results of these actions should be monitored and reentered into the cycle, informing future data collection and analysis.
4. **Strengthening the loop:**
   - To enhance this cycle, businesses should invest in real-time data processing, enabling quicker transitions from data to insights to actions.
   - Equipping staff with the necessary skills and tools to interpret AI-generated insights and implement decisions is critical.
   - Deep integration of AI into business processes ensures that the cycle is not peripheral but central to the operational workflow.
   - Scalability and adaptability of the system are key, allowing businesses to handle growing data volumes and evolving market conditions.

For any business in today's digital age, mastering the data-to-insight-to-action cycle is a cornerstone of success. It is about creating a dynamic, self-improving system where data continuously fuel smarter decisions and more effective actions. This optimized cycle not only enhances operational efficiency but also drives innovation, offering businesses a competitive edge in a rapidly changing marketplace.

The data-to-insight-to-action cycle is crucial in leveraging AI for business value creation, as it transforms vast data into actionable insights, driving informed decision-making and strategic outcomes. This cycle enables companies to respond with agility to market and operational shifts, fostering continuous improvement through AI's evolving learning process. It enhances operational efficiency, risk management, and customer satisfaction, directly contributing to value creation. By harnessing this cycle, businesses can effectively utilize their data assets, innovate, and unlock new growth opportunities, making it a fundamental process in achieving a sustained competitive advantage in today's digital marketplace.

7. Creating Business Value through AI

Business value, in this context, is not just about financial gain. It is a more holistic term, encompassing customer satisfaction, operational efficiency, market differentiation, and innovation potential. So, how exactly does AI fit into this jigsaw of value creation?

- **Direct impact on revenue streams:** AI-driven tools and solutions, like personalized marketing algorithms, have a direct bearing on sales and revenue. They ensure that businesses target the right customers with the right products at the right time, driving sales upward.
- **Operational efficiency:** Automated AI systems streamline processes, minimize human error, and accelerate tasks, resulting in significant cost savings. From supply chain optimizations to human resource management, AI is redefining how businesses operate from the ground up.
- **Enhancing customer experiences:** AI-driven chatbots, recommendation systems, and support tools elevate the customer experience. By offering tailored experiences and instant solutions, businesses not only retain loyal customers but also turn them into brand ambassadors.
- **Innovation and new ventures:** AI unlocks avenues previously unthought-of. It catalyzes product innovations, new service models, and even entire business verticals. Think of how autonomous vehicles are reshaping transport or how AI-driven health diagnostics are revolutionizing healthcare.
- **Risk management:** With predictive analytics and advanced data processing, AI provides businesses with foresight, helping them navigate potential risks. This is invaluable in sectors like

finance, where predicting market movements can make or break fortunes.

- **Sustainability and social impact:** Beyond immediate business metrics, AI aids in long-term sustainability goals. Whether it is optimizing energy consumption in manufacturing or tracking carbon footprints, AI has a role in ensuring businesses thrive without compromising the planet's future.

In tying this back to our narrative, we have understood the rise of data as the new oil, discerned the fundamentals of AI, and plotted strategies for effective data harnessing. Now, with a grasp of how AI creates holistic business value, it is evident that we stand on the precipice of a transformative era. For businesses, the message is clear: Adapt, adopt, and advance with AI, or risk being left behind in a world that waits for no one.

8. Case Studies: Successful Implementations

The power of AI and data analytics becomes most evident when viewed through the prism of real-world applications. Let us illustrate this with two compelling case studies from the railway sector that showcase how predictive maintenance and asset condition monitoring have revolutionized operational efficiency and safety.

8.1. *Railway Predictive Maintenance: From Reactive to Proactive*

Background: Traditionally, railway maintenance is conducted on fixed schedules or in response to evident malfunctions, often leading to operational disruptions and resource-intensive repairs.

Implementation: Leveraging vast amounts of data from sensors installed on tracks, rolling stock (Trains), and infrastructures, Siemens Mobility employed AI-driven predictive models. These models are designed to detect anomalies, predict potential points of failure, and offer insights into parts requiring attention ahead of time. AI models enable the creation of maintenance schedules that are precisely tailored to the individual needs of each train. This customization considers various factors such as the operational history and the current condition of the train as well as typical route demands and environmental factors. For example, a train operating in harsh weather conditions might require more frequent checks on certain components. This bespoke approach ensures maintenance is conducted exactly when needed, enhancing efficiency and prolonging the lifespan of train components. AI systems in predictive maintenance are designed to evolve and improve over time. As the system processes more data, it becomes more adept at identifying patterns and predicting potential issues. This self-improving nature of AI ensures that maintenance strategies become increasingly effective and efficient, reducing errors and enhancing overall system performance. It also helps in identifying long-term trends and wear patterns, contributing to better design and engineering of future rolling stock.

Outcome: The shift from a reactive to a proactive maintenance stance resulted in the following:

- **Cost efficiency:** The shift toward proactive maintenance led to a marked reduction in unplanned maintenance activities. By anticipating and addressing maintenance needs before they escalate into major issues, the maintenance costs were reduced by up to 15%. This represents a substantial cost saving, reflecting the efficiency gains from predictive maintenance strategies.
- **Operational uptime:** The proactive approach in addressing potential disruptions before they escalate has resulted in up to a 40% reduction in costs caused by delays. This enhancement in operational uptime not only improves efficiency but also contributes to better service reliability and customer satisfaction.
- **Enhance availability and reliability:** The optimization of operations through AI-driven insights and predictive models

achieved up to 100% system availability. Additionally, there has been an improvement in system reliability by up to 10%. These figures indicate a remarkable enhancement in the consistency and dependability of railway services, crucial for both passenger and freight operations.

- **Increase capacity digitally:** The integration of asset data, insights, predictive models, and recommendations enabled better network utilization and capacity management. By efficiently managing and utilizing the available resources, the railway network has achieved up to 100% occupancy. This digital increase in capacity signifies not just an optimal use of physical assets but also a smarter way of managing and scheduling railway operations to meet growing demands.

8.2. *Asset Condition Monitoring: Ensuring Optimal Performance*

Background: The vast expanse of railway networks comprises numerous assets, each crucial for seamless operations. Monitoring the condition of these assets manually or through isolated systems is both time-consuming and error-prone.

Implementation: We have adopted an integrated AI-powered asset condition monitoring system. Utilizing data from cameras, vibration sensors, temperature monitors, and many more, our AI-enabled applications offered real-time insights into the condition of assets, from tracks and rolling stock to signals and overhead equipment.

Outcome: This holistic monitoring approach led to the following:

- **Real-time insights:** The integration of AI enabled the immediate detection of asset wear and tear, facilitating prompt intervention. This capability has effectively reduced the frequency of incidents related to asset failure by 50%. Such a reduction not only minimizes disruptions but also contributes to the overall safety and reliability of railway operations.

- **Life cycle extension:** Assets, when monitored and maintained optimally, saw extended operational life, deferring significant replacement costs. The implementation of AI-driven maintenance effectively extended the lifespan of critical train components by 20%, resulting in considerable financial savings. This strategic approach to maintenance, leveraging the predictive capabilities of AI, not only enhances the operational longevity of essential components but also significantly reduces long-term replacement costs
- **Strategic decision-making:** The combination of long-term asset performance data with AI-driven analytics empowers strategic decision-making regarding asset upgrades, replacements, and resource allocation. This informed approach ensures that investments and resources are optimized, aligning with the long-term operational goals and efficiency mandates of the railway system.

The figures presented, although safeguarded for confidentiality, are grounded in realistic cost structures and potential savings derived from these actual case studies. These findings highlight the profound impact of AI and data harnessing within the railway sector. They not only shed light on the tangible advantages in terms of cost efficiency and safety but also underscore the scalability of AI's potential across various industries. For businesses and sectors looking to pivot toward a future-ready stance, such implementations provide both inspiration and a roadmap. The condition-based, predictive maintenance approach through deep understanding and advanced analytics of data from multiple sources enables extended maintenance intervals, eliminates unnecessary work like premature part replacement, and significantly reduces maintenance costs.

9. Challenges and Considerations

As with any transformative technology, the integration of AI into business operations is not without its hurdles. While the previous sections have painted a promising picture of the AI-driven landscape, it is essential to address the challenges and considerations that companies must navigate to harness AI's potential fully.

A leading railway company aimed to integrate AI into its maintenance operations. The objective was to enhance efficiency, safety, and predictability in train operations by using AI for predictive maintenance, fault detection, and operational optimization.

What challenges did they face?

1. **Data quality and integration:**
   - **Challenge:** The company struggled with inconsistent and siloed data from various sources, including train sensors, operational logs, and maintenance records.
   - **Solution:** A centralized data management system was established to standardize and integrate data across different sources, ensuring uniformity and accuracy.
2. **Ethical and privacy concerns:**
   - **Challenge:** Implementing AI raised concerns about data privacy, especially regarding employee and passenger information.
   - **Solution:** The company implemented strict data privacy protocols and anonymized sensitive data before AI processing.
3. **Skills gap in workforce:**
   - **Challenge:** There was a significant skills gap among the workforce regarding AI and data literacy.
   - **Solution:** The company invested in extensive training programs and workshops to upskill employees in AI, data handling, and analytics.
4. **Infrastructure investment:**
   - **Challenge:** Upgrading the existing IT infrastructure to support AI was a substantial financial undertaking.
   - **Solution:** The company opted for a phased investment strategy, gradually building the required infrastructure while demonstrating the ROI from initial deployments.
5. **AI model transparency and explainability:**
   - **Challenge:** Operational staff was skeptical about AI decisions due to the "black box" nature of some AI models.

- **Solution:** The company focused on using AI models that were transparent and provided explainable outputs to gain staff trust.

6. **Regulatory and compliance challenges:**
   - **Challenge:** Adhering to the stringent regulations in the railway industry while implementing AI was complex.
   - **Solution:** A compliance team was established to ensure that all AI integrations were in line with industry regulations and standards.
7. **Scalability and integration issues:**
   - **Challenge:** Integrating AI into existing legacy systems and scaling solutions across the network were challenging.
   - **Solution:** The company collaborated with technology partners for custom AI solutions that were compatible with existing systems and scalable.
8. **Balancing AI and human decision-making:**
   - **Challenge:** There was a concern about overreliance on AI for critical decisions.
   - **Solution:** AI was implemented as a decision support tool rather than a decision-maker, ensuring that human expertise remained central to operational decisions.

Lessons Learned:
1. **Robust data management is crucial:** Effective AI implementation requires high-quality, integrated data.
2. **Prioritize ethics and privacy:** Maintaining ethical standards and data privacy is essential to sustain trust and compliance.
3. **Invest in employee training:** Bridging the AI skills gap through training is critical for successful implementation.
4. **Strategic infrastructure development:** Incremental investment in infrastructure mitigates financial risk and allows for adaptive growth.
5. **Focus on transparent AI:** Transparent and explainable AI models foster trust and acceptance among staff.
6. **Regulatory compliance is essential:** Compliance with industry regulations is non-negotiable and must be a priority.

7. **Collaborate for effective integration:** Partnering with tech providers can facilitate smoother integration and scalability.
8. **Human-centric AI approach:** AI should augment human decision-making, not replace it, especially in critical sectors like railways.

This case study from the railway sector illustrates that while integrating AI into complex operations is challenging, it is achievable with careful planning, ethical considerations, workforce engagement, and strategic investment. The key takeaway is that AI, when implemented thoughtfully and ethically, can significantly enhance operational efficiency and safety in the railway industry.

Addressing these challenges necessitates proactive measures from businesses. Implementing rigorous data governance frameworks can oversee the entire data life cycle, from collection and storage to usage. Tools that validate data can automatically spot and rectify errors. Data augmentation techniques can be used to address data gaps. It is also crucial to audit datasets regularly for biases and rectify them, ensuring AI outputs remain fair. And finally, continuous training and updating of AI models can keep them in sync with the evolving nature of data. The path to AI-driven value creation, while laden with promise, is also fraught with challenges. For businesses, it is not just about celebrating the wins but also about navigating these challenges with foresight and strategic planning. By acknowledging and addressing these considerations head-on, businesses can pave the way for a future where AI augments human potential, driving unprecedented growth and innovation.

10. Future of AI in Business Value Creation

Charting the trajectory of AI in business, it is evident that we are merely at the cusp of realizing its transformative potential. The future beckons with promises of even more profound integrations, innovations, and intersections between AI and business operations. Here's a glimpse into what the horizon might hold:

- **Beyond automation to augmentation:** While the current phase of AI heavily leans toward automation of tasks, the future will see a shift toward augmentation. This means AI will not just replace human tasks but will enhance and elevate human capabilities, leading to collaborations where machines and humans work synergistically. A prime example of this evolution can be observed in the railway industry's approach to predictive maintenance.

  Currently, AI in predictive maintenance primarily automates tasks. It processes data from various sensors on trains and tracks, identifying patterns indicative of wear or potential failure and generating routine maintenance alerts. This automation has led to a more proactive maintenance approach, minimizing unexpected equipment failures and enhancing operational reliability.

  In the future, the role of AI in predictive maintenance is expected to transform, moving toward augmentation. Advanced AI systems will not only perform deeper and broader data analysis, including acoustic, vibration, and high-resolution visual inputs, but will also prescribe specific maintenance actions, optimize repair timings, and dynamically adjust maintenance schedules in real time (*we are already doing this for some of our mobility customers*). This augmented approach will lead to enhanced safety, operational efficiency, and cost savings. Moreover, human roles will evolve from routine task execution to strategic management of AI-enhanced maintenance systems. Engineers and technicians will focus on interpreting AI's insights, implementing strategic decisions, and ensuring quality and safety standards. This paradigm shift will result in a more skilled and strategically focused workforce, enhancing the overall efficiency and effectiveness of the railway industry.

  This example illustrates how the future of AI lies not just in replacing human tasks but in augmenting human abilities, leading to a new era of human–machine collaboration that is more efficient, effective, and synergistic.

- **Hyper-personalization:** With advancements in AI, businesses will be able to offer hyper-personalized experiences to consumers. From tailor-made products to customized user experiences, AI will redefine the benchmarks of personalization.
- **Ethical AI and responsible governance:** As the world grapples with the moral implications of AI decisions, the future will likely see the rise of ethical AI frameworks. These would ensure that AI systems are not just efficient but also fair, transparent, and accountable.
- **Quantum computing and AI:** Quantum computing, with its immense computational power, will push the boundaries of what AI can achieve. Complex problems that are currently beyond AI's reach might become solvable, unlocking new avenues for business value.
- **AI in decision-making hierarchies:** The role of AI will transcend operational levels to influence strategic decision-making. Boardrooms of the future might rely on AI-driven insights to chart out business trajectories, mergers, acquisitions, and more.
- **Democratization of AI:** Tools and platforms will make AI accessible to a broader audience, not just data scientists. This means businesses, irrespective of their size, can leverage AI-driven insights without substantial investments in specialized talent.
- **Evolution of AI-powered ecosystems:** Instead of isolated AI implementations, the future will see interconnected AI ecosystems. These systems will communicate, share insights, and learn from each other, leading to a more holistic and integrated business environment.
- **Continuous learning and adaptability:** Future AI systems will be characterized by their ability to learn continuously and adapt in real time. This ensures that businesses remain agile, adjusting to market dynamics instantaneously.
- **Decentralized AI:** As we move toward a more decentralized web, AI models could become more transparent, customizable,

and privacy-oriented, bringing the power back to individual users and businesses.

- **Neuro-symbolic computing:** A blend of neural networks and symbolic AI, this approach seeks to combine the best of both worlds — the learning capabilities of neural nets and the reasoning capabilities of symbolic AI, potentially transforming decision-making processes in businesses.

As we cast our gaze forward, the realm of AI is poised for profound expansions, setting the stage for unprecedented business value creation. The boundaries of what we understand as AI's capabilities are constantly being redrawn.

The following is a glance at the imminent future, focusing on areas like generative AI and Web 4.0:

- **Generative AI:** Generative AI, an offshoot of machine learning, revolves around models that can generate new, previously unseen content. This extends from creating images and music to generating textual content and design solutions.
  Business Implications:
  o **Product design:** Generative AI can craft innovative designs for products, offering a myriad of options optimized against set parameters, thereby potentially shortening the design phase in industries like automotive, fashion, or electronics.
  o **Content creation:** Industries such as entertainment, advertising, and media could witness a paradigm shift, with AI churning out scripts, music, or even entire movie sequences.
  o **Customization:** From personalized shopping experiences to tailored user interfaces, businesses can leverage generative AI to offer highly individualized experiences, thereby enhancing customer satisfaction and engagement.
  o **Railway infrastructure optimization:** Generative AI can play a significant role in optimizing railway infrastructure design and maintenance. It can generate efficient track layouts, signaling systems, and station designs, helping

railways enhance safety, reduce operational costs, and improve passenger experiences.

- **Web 4.0:** Often termed the "Symbiotic Web," Web 4.0 represents an era where humans and machines coexist in a seamlessly integrated manner. It is not just about machines serving information when queried but proactively understanding and predicting user needs.

Business Implications:

  o **Business intelligence:** With AI-driven analytics on the rise, Web 4.0 will usher in a phase where businesses can draw real-time insights, making on-the-fly adjustments to strategies, whether it is in supply chain management or customer outreach.

  o **Enhanced customer experience:** The era of Web 4.0 will see businesses offering not just reactive but also predictive customer support. Imagine a scenario where customer issues are addressed even before customers are fully aware of them.

  o **Integrated workflows:** Businesses will experience heightened collaboration and integration across departments, with AI seamlessly connecting dots, identifying gaps, and suggesting optimizations in real time.

In this envisioned future, AI emerges not as a mere tool but as an integral fabric of business operations. The symbiotic relationship between AI and business will deepen, setting the stage for an era where value creation is not just about profitability but also about enhancing human potential, fostering innovation, and ushering in a paradigm of responsible and equitable growth.

As these technological wonders become a part of our daily business lexicon, the imperative lies in continuous learning, adaptation, and integration, ensuring that businesses are not just consumers of this technology but pioneers leading the charge. The horizon of business value creation is expanding, and it is a future filled with immense promise.

11. Conclusion

The intersection of AI and business is an exhilarating frontier, rich with opportunities and challenges alike. Throughout this chapter, we have journeyed from understanding the fundamental drivers, such as the ascendancy of data, to delving deep into how AI is transforming the landscape of business value creation. Through real-world case studies, we have seen tangible manifestations of this potential, and looking ahead, the horizon promises even more profound integrations and innovations.

Yet, it is crucial to approach this frontier with a balanced perspective. The promise of AI is undeniable, but its successful implementation demands meticulous strategy, ethical considerations, and continuous adaptability. It is not just about harnessing computational power but aligning it with human insights, values, and aspirations.

The future of AI in business is not just a narrative of machines and algorithms; it is a story of enhanced human potential. It is about leveraging technology to address age-old business challenges, to unlock novel opportunities, and to forge a path of sustainable, inclusive growth. In this milieu, businesses do not just thrive; they evolve, adapt, and redefine the paradigms of success.

As we stand at this pivotal juncture, the imperative is clear. Embrace AI, not as a mere tool, but as a partner in this journey. Let it augment our capabilities, elevate our aspirations, and guide us toward a future where business value is both tangible and transformative. The scales are tipped, and the onus is on us to harness this momentum, charting a course into a promising, AI-augmented future.

Successful AI and data initiatives rely on a strategic approach that aligns with the organization's overarching goals. It is crucial to define specific business problems that AI aims to solve, ensuring a clear connection between AI projects and strategic objectives. Additionally, maintaining data quality and governance is paramount. Clean and well-managed data form the foundation for effective AI projects, emphasizing the importance of robust data quality assurance processes.

Finally, strengthening the data-to-insight-to-action loop is pivotal, as it bridges the gap between AI insights and actionable business decisions, ultimately creating value from AI investments. This process serves as the bridge that connects AI-generated insights to actionable business decisions, enabling organizations to translate data-driven findings into tangible value.

In essence, this loop ensures that AI insights do not remain isolated observations but are transformed into strategic actions that drive business outcomes. It involves developing clear and efficient processes for taking the insights generated by AI models and implementing them in decision-making and operational activities. By closing this loop effectively, organizations can unlock the true transformative power of AI, driving efficiency, innovation, and competitive advantage in their respective industries.

Chapter 12

Using AI to Power a Digital Bank with a Human Touch

Chalee Asavathiratham*

Siam Commercial Bank, Bangkok, Thailand
chalee.asavathiratham@scb.co.th

Abstract

This chapter discusses Siam Commercial Bank's journey toward transforming itself from a large traditional bank into a digital bank that blends AI capabilities with a human touch. As a bank, we had faith in both the power of AI and the "undigitizable" qualities that human banking agents can bring to our customers — trust, empathy, and professionalism, among others. By using our capabilities in data analytics and AI to deliver a hybrid AI–human service model, we believe we can differentiate ourselves and best serve our customers' needs. While our transformation is far from over, it is worth reflecting on the key lessons that we have gathered thus far. Our hope is that business leaders can apply these lessons to guide their future digitization projects. We first describe our background and motivation, then move on to the key steps along the value chain — customer acquisition, data

*With gratitude to Dr. Arnon Tonmukayakul, Anak Tangtatswas, and Dr. Natawat Saigosoom for their great contribution to this chapter.

monetization, and digital services. Finally, we conclude with some of the key learnings from our journey.

Keywords: Digital transformation, digital banking, digital revenue, digital underwriting, omnichannel banking, data and analytics in banking, digital services, hybrid human–digital banking.

1. Background and Motivation

Siam Commercial Bank (SCB), founded over a century ago, is the first bank and one of the largest in Thailand. As a leading bank, we have gone through multiple transformations throughout our history, the latest being a data-led transformation that began in 2017 when we invested substantially in our data infrastructure and analytics capabilities.

These investments coincided with the market-wide shift toward the digital channel as the preferred mode among customers. While the number of digital users in the Thai market has been steadily increasing, the pace significantly picked up during the COVID-19 pandemic. As of mid-2023, over 90% of banking customers have adopted digital channels and transaction volumes continue to grow at a rate of over 20% annually. Against this backdrop, our relative head start in data infrastructure along with the rapid adoption of the digital channels gives us the perfect opportunity to drive significant value from AI.

1.1. *Evolution of the Data Team*

1.1.1. *Episode 1 — Data as the rearview mirror*

A data team was constituted that was regarded as a part of the Information Technology team. To begin with, SCB utilized data to provide a quantitative reflection of "what has happened." For this, we incorporated data into the creation of various reports and dash-boards, as well as various business intelligence tools.

From Data to Digital Banking: Three Episodes of SCB AI Evolution 

Fig. 1. Evolution of the SCB's data and AI capabilities.

While such use cases are useful in informing the various business units and the management in tracking how the bank is doing, they do not fully harness the power of prediction embedded in the data. During that phase, much of the discussion about data centered on data lakes, data engineering, or computer infrastructure. The creation of a data lake was a massive undertaking for a universal bank that has grown organically over the years. The data lake was incrementally built and was a consolidation of clean, curated customer and operational data from approximately 700 applications. A few hundred engineers worked on this transformation project that ported the data into a single storage infrastructure in the cloud.

1.1.2. *Episode 2 — Data on the front line*

As the bank built its data science capabilities, data were used more to make predictions and derive more business value. The data team separated from the IT team and began to realign itself with the goal of data monetization. The most common use cases at the time included lead generation or providing the sales team with a list of high-potential customers to call, the use of propensity models or

AI models to predict the likelihood of a customer purchasing a certain product based on a large number of attributes, developing underwriting models or using AI to help decide whether to approve a loan, and finding out when and how to remind a customer that their payment is due, to name a few.

While the data capabilities greatly improved the productivity of our operations, we soon realized that our operating model could improve further. Being a part of the IT team meant that the data team was only operating in a passive mode by responding to requests from the business units that interfaced with the customers. Being one step removed from the customers prevents the data team from understanding the real pain points that customers face and testing innovative solutions directly.

With this insight, the data team graduated into the digital banking team, and turned from a supporting function into an independent business unit with its own business goal. We began launching a niche line of digital loans for both consumers and small businesses. At that point in time, data had been moved from a back-end activity to the "front line" of the business. The short feedback loop between the digital banking team and the customers allowed the team to test and iterate new product ideas more rapidly, instead of having to rely on an external go-between.

1.1.3. *Episode 3 — Data as the enabler of a digital bank with a human touch*

New products and services emerged as we immersed AI into the design process. For instance, we eliminated the income verification process for many of our business customers by using the AI-based proxy income. This reduced the time for a loan application from days to just minutes for hundreds of customers. As the use case for data monetization in the bank grew, we began to ask bigger questions. Instead of just using data to deliver value through digital products, can we also use it more broadly to improve our customer experience? Can we provide our customers with a seamless omnichannel experience using data? Thus began our quest to blend the digital and offline experience. Instead of treating digital products as distinct from traditional products, we embedded AI into all our products and services. Instead of treating our channel as either digital or offline, we combined the two together and built an omnichannel delivery strategy using proxy income as described earlier. We are now determined to use our data as the driving force toward our goal of becoming a digital bank with a human touch.

1.2. *Why a Human Touch?*

Our decision to combine a human touch with our digital capabilities stems from a few reasons. First, our bank wants to differentiate itself from new purely digital entrants in the banking space by offering a superior experience to our customers via our human staff. Second, the bank wants to focus on customers in the middle segments and above. In particular, we want to become the best-known bank for digital wealth, an area that requires significant trust from our clients. We believe that servicing customers in this segment via strictly digital channels may fail to deliver service attributes that only a human touch can provide, namely, trust, empathy, and professionalism. Third, we believe that our advancements in data analytics and AI need not be limited to digital channels. A proper hybrid mode of AI and human interactions can boost the quality and productivity of our customer interactions. For example, we can use AI to guide which conversation topics a relationship manager should have with his or her customer.

1.3. *The Need for Future-Proofing*

The need to mix digital and offline channels coincides with the arrival of virtual banks in Thailand. As of the time of writing this chapter, the Bank of Thailand has announced that it will grant up to three new virtual bank licenses and anticipates the grantees to start their operations in 2025. The prospect of competing with virtual banks that are potentially much more technologically advanced gives us a new sense of urgency. Not only do we have to lower our cost but we also must differentiate ourselves from the purely digital ones.

1.4. *How We Approach Digital Banking with a Human Touch*

To realize the concept of digital banking with a human touch, we developed a three-pronged approach focusing on the following three areas by asking pointed questions relevant to each of the functions:

(i) **Acquisition:** Can we use AI to minimize our customer acquisition cost? Can we seamlessly blend AI capabilities with our human-based acquisition?

(ii) **Monetization:** Once the customers are onboard, how can we use our data to generate the most value for our customers, thereby allowing us to monetize from those relations?

(iii) **Service:** Can we use data and analytics to lower the cost to serve and increase customer satisfaction?

These areas will be discussed in detail in the following sections.

2. Digital Acquisition: Journey toward AI-Driven "Customer-Centric" Engagement

At SCB, we strive to make the best use of data to deliver the best customer experience to our customers while also driving value to the bank. Prior to the digital transformation, customer acquisition was largely product based. Sales targets were driven mainly by trying to maximize the *frequency* of reaching our customers, by sending as many marketing messages across digital and offline channels as each Business Unit is allowed. Even though we consistently delivered solid financial results, our marketing messages received low single-digit click-through rates on digital channels. Consequently, customers were often overwhelmed with uncoordinated marketing messages. They perceived digital marketing channels to be more about what the bank wants to focus on rather than about what the customers truly needed. This challenge also caused a "channel fatigue" effect, leading customers to ignore or block the digital channels altogether over time.

With our aspiration of becoming a "digital bank with a human touch," we set our goal to increase our digital revenue from 5% to 25% within 3 years. However, we realized that without the extensive use of data and digital to transform the way we work, we would not be able to truly become the "digital bank with a human touch" that we aspired to be, even if we achieved our financial goals. This prompted us to come up with a new customer-centric engagement model powered by data and AI to not only drive financial results but also transform the way we work and engage with our customers.

2.1. *The Beginning of "Digital Acquisition": AI-Power Digital Engagement*

At the start of the journey, we focused on using data and AI to drive better engagement in digital channels. We focused our initial efforts on the SCB Connect platform, a chat-based communication channel on the LINE chat application with over 10 million customers. SCB Connect is our main marketing channel through which we have sent over 50 million marketing messages on a monthly basis and have the high agility to deploy data models and perform A/B testing with a quick feedback loop.

To come up with data models to engage the customers at the right time and moment, we arranged multiple brainstorming sessions with product and customer experience teams to jointly identify opportunities. Our data analysts then developed various models and tested the results with our customers with an active feedback loop. We would orchestrate a large number of comparison tests (A/B testing) of new features that we wanted to introduce. Once a new feature was confirmed to be superior to the old ones, we used that feature as the new baseline and built upon it. There were different types of models that were deployed to drive our digital acquisition.

One example of our AI models is a personalized product recommendation engine. From the historic application rate of 0.35%, our data analytics team developed a propensity model to match the loan offerings to the right customers, driving the application rate to 2.2%. To improve the engagement even further, we analyzed the best time to engage with our clients, analyzing their application usage across different days and times to personalize when to best reach out to each customer. The results were an even further uplift with a 4.3% application rate. Taking a step further, in addition to knowing the propensity to apply and the best time to engage, the team then explored the right artwork and messages to engage with each customer. We found that with the right personalization, we could even drive the application rate to 4.8%, a 14x enhancement compared to the traditional way of working. All of these were made possible through a collaboration between data analytics, businesses, customer experience, and platform teams working closely together through active discussion and feedback loops.

Trying to put our customers at the center, we also identified opportunities to best engage them with "a human touch" by sending them insights they cared about at the right time and moment. One example is our Just4U platform, a personal finance hub for our customers. We adopted AI to assist customers in auto-tracking their inflow and outflow transactions, doing auto-categorization of transactions and delivering personalized insights such as tax planning advice to help propel our customers toward better financial well-being. Within 8 months, we launched over 120 insights and achieved over 2.4x more engaged users. Our personalized "Happy Birthday" messages bundled with product promotions also received 15x more engagement compared with traditional marketing messages.

Our results have shown that with data and AI, we can provide a tremendous uplift to our businesses while also increasing our customer engagement and satisfaction. However, to truly become a digital bank with a human touch, we started to explore ways to deploy our models beyond our digital channel and empower our human touchpoints with AI-based insights, leading to our new journey toward "customer-centric operating model."

2.2. *Powering Human with AI — The Next Chapter*

We envision the future of banking to be AI-driven, yet with a human touch. What this means is to have an AI brain at the center of all customer interactions, digital and non-digital. Our workforce should have the full context of our customer needs, potential value, and journeys. We should understand each customer's wants, how much value they can bring to the bank, what they have engaged with, and what interactions they have been through across our touchpoints. These contexts should then be dynamically translated into the next steps and best actions to engage with the customers at the right time and moment. We want to deliver a hyper-personalized experience to our customers wherever they choose to engage with us, either through digital channels or through our digital-empowered human touchpoints.

To turn this grand vision into reality, we embarked on a dual-track approach, piloting quick executable components to build momentum while building an integrated roadmap toward the future of banking. Realizing the full value of data and AI requires not just models and algorithms but also human insights and new ways of working. For example, in order to put AI at the center of customer interactions, we would need to realign sales incentives and break the traditional boundaries around how we perceive segments, products, and channels.

We have embarked on a multi-year journey by segmenting our customers into over 1,000 microsegments based on financial and behavioral data. Our proprietary data models also predicted the potential value of each of our 18 million customers based on advanced underwriting and propensity models. Our journey toward a "customer-centric operating model" is based on the prioritization of these microsegments which will guide us on which components across people, processes, and platforms to enable first. Active cross-functional collaboration to blend human insights into our AI models and our agile test-and-learn approach will help us adapt and refine both our AI models and our way of working toward our aspired future state.

We may have realized a lot of value from data and AI to date, but we are even more excited now about the potential we are yet to tap into from the upcoming journeys toward becoming a "digital bank with a human touch."

3. Data Monetization

With customer behavior having shifted toward online transactions, digital behavior, i.e., digital footprint, is easier to track and hence generates a vast amount of data. The data are, however, meaningless without ways of generating real financial returns. In other words, data are only as useful as the analytics and applications, which also means the correlation of data and causation analysis is key to producing return on data investment.

3.1. *The Virtuous Cycle of Customers, Data, and Moments*

Although banking is a heavily regulated industry, banks may have advantages in terms of compliance, security, and number of customers. Yet, they may lack enterprise agility and flexibility when compared to Fintech firms. This becomes a challenge, especially when trying to meet the demand of customers who are less receptive to mass offerings. Tailored experiences and personalized offerings are inevitably becoming standard across industry verticals.

To ensure that a bank can cater to the needs of its customers, it is imperative that the bank remain highly proactive in providing personalized products and services that are tailored to the specific requirements of each customer. This can be achieved by leveraging customer data to gain a deeper understanding of customer preferences and needs, and delivering these products and services through the right channels at the right time with the right message. By doing so, the bank can establish a strong relationship with its

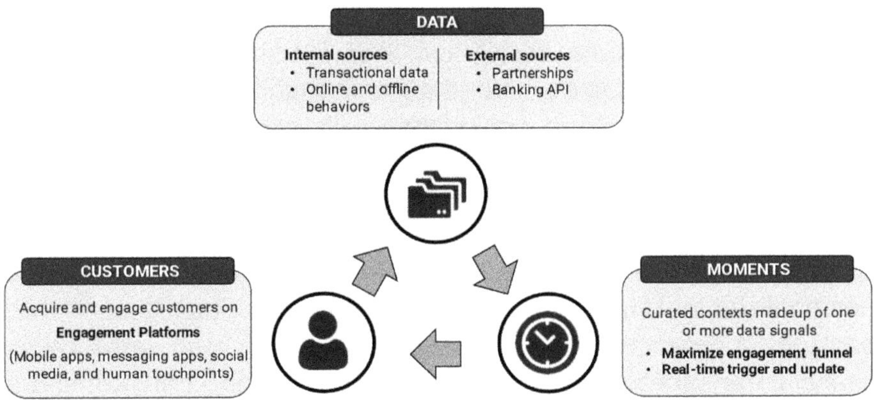

Fig. 2.   The virtuous cycle of customers, data, and moments.

customers, which will ultimately lead to greater customer satisfaction and loyalty.

To become a personalized, AI-first bank, it is essential to overhaul the suboptimal operating model. The key to delivering data monetization benefits lies in driving personalization at scale and maintaining rapid innovation cycles. Figure 2 shows the cycle of three components that enable valuable data for monetization.

Customers: Platforms and products are instrumental in driving customer engagement, which can take various forms such as product onboarding, service transactions, complaints, and browsing behavior. The design of products and user experience on the platform plays a crucial role in determining the quality of data generated.

Data: Internal data sources, which encompass transactional data and digital behavior, and external data sources, which are derived from partnerships and services provided to external parties, are both valuable sources of data. Effective management and prioritization of these data sources are essential for cost and quality management, and identifying data elements should be in real time. Further details on this topic will be provided in the next section.

Moments: Data are utilized to generate signals, which are essentially a combination of data correlation and causation with business understanding. This is developed through machine learning. These signals are then used in conjunction with other preferences and parameters to define the moment to trigger actions. These actions could be either selling, nurturing, servicing, or retaining.

A prime example of how these three components work together is the personalized investment product recommendation feature on mobile banking applications. By providing "customers" with easy-to-use financial transactions (such as payment, top-up, and transfer) and a spending summary for their daily life, along with a comprehensive investment portfolio performance, the app platform generates engagement and hence clickstream "data" that signify interest in specific investment products (such as mutual funds, bonds, and special savings). The data also show behavior at different points of time, such as app log-on patterns, and key triggers for certain actions over time, such as the moment of interest in investment products right after fund inflow. These data points are then used to identify "moments" to engage customers with sell triggers of investment products.

Using these data points, the app has observed an almost 14 times uplift in sale conversion rate compared to mass marketing methods. An uplift of 6 times can be attributed to targeted product offering through feature engineering of engagement data. Another uplift of 6 times is due to using the right moment to sell from signals such as fund flow trigger and app usage behavior. Finally, personalized artwork and messages to capture attention based on the customer's situation generate another uplift of 1.5 times.

3.2. *Path to Data Monetization*

To optimize data utilization for both revenue generation and cost savings, we employ the approach illustrated in Fig. 3. This approach involves the following steps:

1. **High-value data acquisition:** To generate high-value data for business, it is essential to establish a data valuation methodology

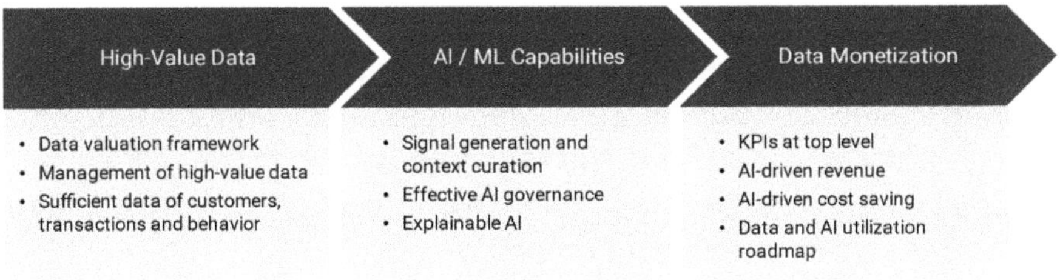

Fig. 3.   Data monetization.

framework that can help identify the data areas that are most valuable. This can be achieved by back-testing predictive power with business use cases for different machine learning feature sets, which enables us to estimate their financial value and rank them accordingly. By doing so, organizations can develop a strategy to prioritize resources for the acquisition and management of these datasets.

In certain scenarios, this approach can also aid in rationalizing investments in products and services that generate valuable data. For instance, product features that attract engagement traffic from users may not directly generate revenue, but they can produce high-value datasets that reveal customer interests, intentions, lifestyles, and locations. These datasets can be leveraged for monetization purposes at a later stage. The crux of the matter is to establish a link between financial value and these engagement data.

2. **AI and ML capabilities:** To leverage the data available to us, we employ a variety of AI and ML capabilities to predict and generate accurate signals that can trigger the sale, service, nurture, or retain action. These real-time signals are generated to identify the most effective course of action.

   It is possible that the suggested actions may need to be carried out by humans. Unlike traditional methods of defining work processes, machine learning-generated actions may be questioned for their accuracy and legitimacy. Therefore, it is imperative that we apply AI governance and explainable AI principles. This is to ensure that the machine suggestions are transparent, trustworthy, and fair and maintain customer privacy. It also allows stakeholders such as customers, salespersons, service agents, and regulators to understand how decisions are made and the rationale behind them. In turn, this will help us build trust with our stakeholders and foster a culture of transparency and accountability.

3. **Data monetization KPIs:** To ensure that the business is aligned with its strategic goal of becoming a data-driven organization, we apply measurable KPIs of data monetization from the top of the organization. These KPIs include AI-driven revenue and AI-driven cost savings, which are essential for optimizing data utilization and driving business growth. By leveraging these KPIs, we can establish a clear roadmap for achieving our organizational objectives and ensure that our actions are always aligned with our long-term vision.

4. The Power of Digital Services at SCB

In today's rapidly evolving banking landscape, the role of digital services has emerged as a pivotal factor in shaping the success of financial institutions. SCB stands at the forefront of this digital revolution, leveraging innovative technologies to enhance customer experience, drive value, optimize operations, and secure a commanding position in this highly competitive industry.

4.1. *Enhanced Customer Experience*

At the heart of SCB's digital service strategy lies an unwavering commitment to providing an exceptional customer experience. The integration of user-friendly interfaces, personalized financial services, and real-time support creates an environment where customers can seamlessly navigate their banking needs with unprecedented ease and convenience. Through the application of cutting-edge technologies such as artificial intelligence and machine learning, SCB empowers customers with tailored insights and services.

This is exemplified through two key channels: SCB Easy, the bank's mobile banking platform, and SCB Connect, a line messaging app designed to provide instant financial alerts and services.

The level of individualized attention afforded to each customer not only fosters trust but also establishes a new benchmark for customer-centricity within the banking industry. It is worth noting that the Net Promoter Score (NPS) serves as one of the primary metrics employed by the bank to gauge customer experience, reflecting the institution's dedication to measuring and improving satisfaction levels.

4.2. *Increasing Customer Value*

At SCB, digital services transcend the mere enhancement of customer experience; they drive quantifiable increases in customer value. Swift issue resolution and personalized interactions on digital platforms cultivate higher levels of satisfaction, resulting in a positive impact on the overall customer experience. As customer satisfaction rises, so does the likelihood of customers evolving into loyal advocates, becoming enthusiastic proponents of the bank's services, and in turn acting as organic catalysts for business growth.

The associated relationship between customer experience and value is illustrated in Figs. 4 and 5. These visual representations underscore the correlation between customer experience, as measured by the Net Promoter Score (NPS),[1] and the Assets Under Management (AUM) in monetary units at SCB. Significantly, promoters, who are ardent supporters of the bank, exhibit a markedly higher rate of AUM growth compared to passive and detractor customers, which holds true for both the retail and wealth segments.

---

[1] Respondents rate from 0 (not likely) to 10 (extremely likely), categorizing them into Promoters (9–10), Passives (7–8), and Detractors (0–6) to calculate NPS. Promoters are loyal and enthusiastic, Passives are satisfied but not enthusiastic, while Detractors are unhappy and unlikely to repurchase (Qualtrics, 2023).

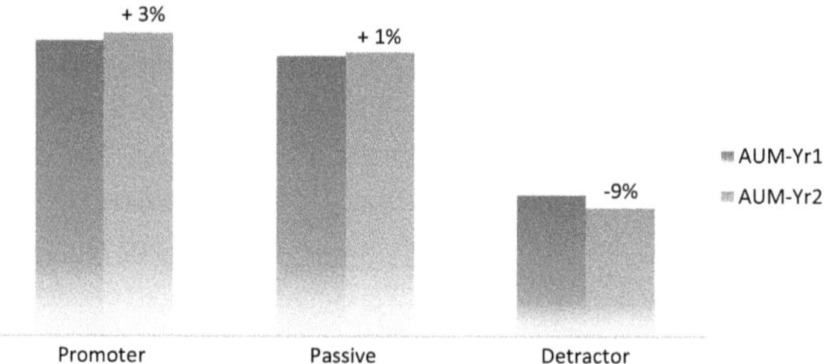

Fig. 4. A comparison between Net Promoter Score and Assets Under Management of SCB's retail customers over a two-year period. The *Y*-axis represents the monetary unit, while the *X*-axis represents the Net Promoter segments. The percentage change illustrates the movement of AUM between the two consecutive years.

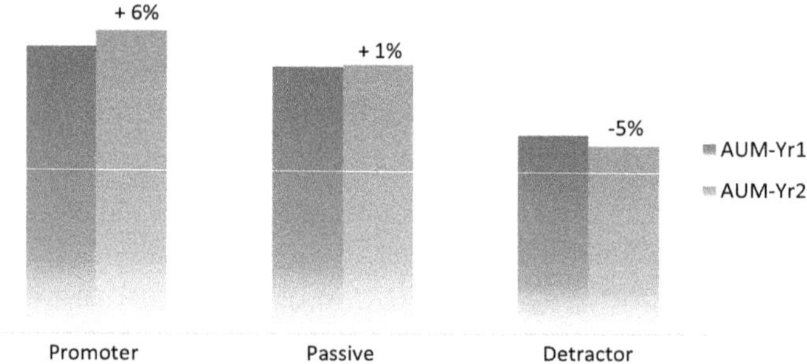

Fig. 5. A comparison between Net Promoter Score and Assets Under Management of SCB's wealth customers over a two-year period. The *Y*-axis represents the monetary unit, while the *X*-axis represents the Net Promoter segments. The percentage change illustrates the movement of AUM between the two consecutive years.

4.3. *Optimizing Cost to Serve*

In an industry where, striking a balance between profitability and delivering value to customers is crucial, prioritizing cost efficiency is of paramount importance. SCB's strategic investments in digital service channels have proven instrumental in yielding substantial benefits in this area. The implementation of Robotic Process Automation (RPA) for automating routine transactions, offering self-service options, and integrating chatbot technology has resulted in a significant reduction in operational costs previously tied to traditional physical touchpoints.

This streamlined digital service infrastructure not only lowered costs but also enabled the redirection of resources toward customer-centric operating model interactions. As a result, this has enhanced operational efficiency and increased cost-effectiveness. Notably, in 2023, SCB introduced "Alert Now" to proactively communicate money transfer errors on SCB Easy to affected customers and "Download Now" to digitize auto and home loan documents available on digital channels. SCB is set to leverage ChatGPT to reduce fallback rates when chatbots are unable to understand user inputs, thereby improving the chatbot experience for customer service. These strategic initiatives culminated in an almost 6% reduction in cost to serve compared to the previous year.

In today's competitive banking landscape, the adoption of digital services has become a key differentiator and a fundamental driver of success. By prioritizing customer experience, managing customer values, optimizing cost efficiency, and embracing digital channels, SCB has not only elevated its standing in digital services but also established a formidable competitive edge. This strategic approach resonates with today's digitally empowered consumers, solidifying SCB's position as a leader in the industry.

5. Lessons Learnt

There are many challenges that we face along our AI journey, and we are constantly working through new ones every day. Some of them are more specific to our historical structure and may not be applicable to an organization with a different structure or legacy structure.

5.1. *AI and Humans are Good at Different Things — Blend their Capabilities*

Despite all the advances in analytics and AI, a bank can only operate if the customers trust it. High-value, complex transactions will still require a human touch. Customers might be comfortable making small transactions online, but for a more complex transaction that requires "trust" such as a 20-year insurance policy or a 30-year home mortgage, they want to know that there is someone they can trust behind such a transaction. From our experiences, we have learned that we should use AI to serve our customers in lower-value, higher-frequency types of interactions so that our salespersons and our relationship managers can focus their time on understanding our customers, answering queries from customers, and building trust with them. We should not aim to replace those human interactions completely but rather supercharge their productivity through AI-driven useful tools.

5.2. *Friction is Exponentially Expensive*

One of the big lessons we learned from building digital banking applications is that every extra step on our applications represents an attrition in customer acquisition; every extra field to fill leads to a drop-off. The cumulative effect of a long loan application, for example, is a drop-off that increases exponentially as the application form lengthens. We, therefore, employ AI and analytics to pre-qualify our customers so that their applications can be as frictionless as possible.

5.3. *Attract High-Value Traffic*

"Build it and they will come" used to be the mantra of many companies at the start of digital transformation. Hoping to recreate the network effect of early platform-based companies such as Facebook, LinkedIn, and Uber that have experienced a positive feedback loop — a large customer base drawing in even more customers — companies are willing to invest in customer acquisition and grow aggressively despite the lack of clarity on the paths toward revenue. In banking, we have learned that customer traffic can have vastly different values. While the cost for serving the most profitable group of customers is comparable to that of serving the least profitable ones, their revenue potential can differ by several orders of magnitude. Whenever possible, one should, therefore, focus on acquiring high-value customers with a clear path to monetization rather than acquiring a customer base indiscriminately.

5.4. *Data are Not the New Oil — Correlation Is*

It is commonly said that data is the new oil, which implies that one should acquire as much data as possible. However, we feel that such a viewpoint misses the fact that what we really want from data is the power to predict the future. In turn, prediction capabilities come from the amount of correlation that one can extract from the data. In that sense, data is the *new crude oil*. Every company should focus on acquiring more correlation, not just acquiring more data per se.

5.5. *Our Journey Continues...*

As Jeff Bezos would put it, "It is still Day 1" of our journey toward creating a digital bank with a human touch. At the time of writing this in December 2023, the bank is enjoying a record year in all key measures — highest profit, lowest cost-to-income ratio, and highest customer satisfaction — but this is hardly the time for us to remain complacent. The true test is yet to come. New digital banks are entering the Thai banking industry and new disruptive technologies such as generative AI are constantly emerging to surprise us with their capabilities. Through these new waves of changes, we will learn, adapt, and strive. A century ago, SCB was founded as the first bank in Thailand. A century from now, we will hopefully be remembered as the first bank to have found the optimal balance in blending new technologies with the right amount of human touch.

Chapter 13

Generative AI Output for Business Organizations: Legal Perspectives from Copyright Law

Hannah Yee-Fen Lim

Nanyang Business School, Nanyang Technological University, 91 Nanyang Avenue, ABS-06-072, Singapore
yeefen@ntu.edu.sg

Abstract

The aim of this chapter is to critically analyze the legal landscape of the use of generative AI under copyright law in major jurisdictions, enabling readers to harness the benefits of generative AI while minimizing exposure to undue legal liability and risks. In many jurisdictions, the raw output of generative AI systems may not be protected under copyright law as an intangible asset. However, if some effort is made to alter the output that demonstrates that some skill or judgment has been applied, then the organization or business will be able to claim copyright over the amended output and incorporate the use and value of the copyright in their organization or business.

Keywords: Artificial intelligence, generative AI, copyright law, business valuation, AI-generated output.

1. Introduction

Artificial Intelligence (AI) systems might be good servants, but they are dangerous masters. The aim of this chapter is to critically analyze the legal landscape of the use of generative AI under copyright law, enabling readers to harness the benefits of generative AI while minimizing exposure to undue legal liability and risks. Generative AI systems have reached a level of sophistication where they can produce seemingly useful output in the form of text, images, audios, and audiovisuals.

The quality of the output of such AI systems has reached a stage where it can be commercially helpful to businesses, including increasing productivity. While text and chat-based generative AI systems such as ChatGPT and Bard have consistently been in mainstream news, text-to-image generative AI systems such as Midjourney, DALL-E, and Stable Diffusion have also been highly utilized to produce not just literary but also dramatic and artistic works. There has also been an explosion in generative AI systems for music and musical works such as Loudly, Audiocraft, Boomy, MuseNet, Soundful, and Soundraw. All these tools can be tapped into by organizations for their commercial needs. But are they legally sound to use?

2. Copyright as a Key Intangible Asset

Generative AI can generate value through the creation of intangible assets such as copyright for organizations. Copyright in turn helps organizations protect other intangible assets, such as website presence and content, trademarks, branding, product designs, and marketing and promotional materials. The licensing of copyright-protected materials can also create new revenue streams for organizations. With so much digital information being created and distributed by organizations in the current digital era, copyright protection is essential.

Generative AI systems enable organizations to be more productive through time, resource, and cost savings in the creation of key business and organizational processes and infrastructures and to leapfrog the competition in many aspects of business operations.

2.1. *Copyright Law and the Output of Generative AI*

The short answer as to whether generative AI can create or co-create intellectual property is both yes and no. Much depends on the particular and material facts of the situation of the value creation.

The subject matter of copyright is quite varied and includes the following[1]:

(1) literary works;
(2) dramatic works;
(3) artistic works, including drawings, paintings, photographs, etchings, sculptures, buildings and models of buildings, and works of artistic craftsmanship;
(4) musical works, including any accompanying words;
(5) cinematograph films and other audiovisual works;
(6) sound recordings;
(7) television and sound broadcasts;
(8) qualifying performances; and
(9) published editions of literary, dramatic, musical, or artistic works.

All of these carry value in their own right and some can be derivatives of others. For example, a novel is a protected literary work upon which a cinematograph film can be made, which in turn is protected by a separate copyright, but both the novel and the film are of economic value. A company may use a song as part of its branding. The song may be protected by several copyrights: the copyright in the lyrics, which is a literary work; the copyright in the

---

[1] See, for example, Copyright Act 1968 (Australia) Sections 32, 89–92 and Copyright Act 2021 (Singapore) Sections 9, 21, 24, 28, 34.

music score, which is a musical work; and finally, the song as it is played and sung, which is a sound recording. All of these are of value to a business.

The essential prerequisite before any work can be a subject matter of copyright protection is that it needs to be expressed because copyright only protects the expression of ideas, not the ideas themselves. Ideas alone cannot be protected. Copyright owners have the exclusive right to control specific uses and commercial exploitation of their works for a limited period of time; the amount of time depends on the type of copyrighted works. This also means that copyright owners have the right to prevent others from doing the things only the copyright owner has the right to do, such as reproducing, publishing, performing, communicating to the public, or adapting the work.

This chapter will focus largely on the major types of works covered by copyright that is relevant for most businesses, namely, literary, dramatic, artistic, and musical works. These types of works are the most commonly found copyrighted materials in the arsenal of essential intangible assets of business organizations. For example, most businesses would have company logos and photographs that are protected by copyright. If any marketing is undertaken, the marketing materials could be literary and artistic works. Larger firms may develop audio-visual advertisements and these would trigger literary, artistic, dramatic and musical works, and films, which are constructed out of the literary, artistic and musical works. Internal to the organizational processes, many documents and items may be protected as literary or artistic works.

2.2. *Copyright Law — No Human Input*

An organization may utilize generative AI but the output generated may not necessarily always be protected by copyright. Nevertheless, even if the output may not be protected by copyright, it can still be utilized to the benefit of the organization. The following sections will explore the circumstances under which generative AI can be put to create value.

Works generated *solely* by a machine or an AI system may not be protected by copyright because the copyright legislation in many countries specifies that there needs to be human involvement in order for copyright protection to subsist.

This is the case in Australia, where section 31 of the Copyright Act specifies that only a "person" can be the author of a literary, dramatic, musical, or artistic work. While sections 89 to 92 and 96 to 100AH covering other types of copyrighted materials do not always have direct reference to "person," these provisions do imply that the maker and owner of the copyright need to be a legal person, such as a company, that is recognized by law. These provisions use the terminology of "maker" coupled with references to "person" and "persons," which renders it very difficult to apply to AI systems. Generative AI tools are not legal persons recognized by law, hence in Australia, they cannot be the owners or creators of copyrighted materials.

The situation is similar in Singapore. Many provisions imply that creators of literary, dramatic, musical, or artistic works need to be human to qualify for protection. For example, the copyright protection duration is pegged to the death of a person,[2] suggesting that the copyright creator needs to be a human. Much of Singapore's copyright legislation, like Australia's, also refers to "maker" peppered with references to "person" for the other types of copyrighted materials.

In the United States, the legal position is also similar, with the precursor to the modern law, the 1909 Copyright Act, explicitly expressing that only a "person" could be the copyright owner.[3] Further, the US position is confirmed by at least one court case and two decisions of the United States Copyright Office. In the case of *Thaler v Perlmutter*[4] in the US District Court, the plaintiff Thaler sought to claim copyright over a work that was autonomously

---

[2] Copyright Act 2021 (Singapore) Sections 114–115.

[3] Copyright Act 1909 (US) Act of March 4, 1909, Chapter 320, Sections 9, 10, 35 Stat. 1075, 1077.

[4] *Thaler v Perlmutter.* (2023). 1:22-cv-01564-BAH (ECF #24), D.D.C. August 18, 2023.

created by a computer algorithm. Thaler filed his lawsuit against the United States Copyright Office and Shira Perlmutter, in her official capacity as the Register of Copyrights and the Director of the United States Copyright Office ("Defendants"), as the Defendants had rejected Thaler's copyright application on the grounds that the work lacked human authorship, a prerequisite for a valid copyright to subsist. In the August 2023 decision, the District Court agreed with the Defendants.

In a separate decision, the US Copyright Office had registered a copyright, only to rescind it later when it discovered that the work was the result of generative AI. In September 2022, Kris Kashtanova received copyright registration for a graphic novel created with images generated by Midjourney, a generative AI program. In October 2022, the Copyright Office initiated cancellation proceedings, where it noted that Kashtanova had not disclosed the use of AI, a fact pertinent to the question of originality. On February 21, 2023, the Copyright Office determined that the images were not copyrightable as Kashtanova was not the author because they were generated by a generative AI system.[5]

In a more recent September 2023 decision, the US Copyright Office again rejected copyright protection for art created using generative AI. Jason M. Allen had won the Colorado State Fair's art competition in 2022 for an image he created using Midjourney. When he tried to apply for copyright protection, he claimed that he had input numerous revisions and text prompts, at least 624 times, into Midjourney and then altered the image with Adobe Photoshop. The US Copyright Office asked Allen to disclaim the parts of the image that Midjourney generated in order to receive copyright protection. However, Allen declined and hence his application for copyright was rejected by the U.S. Copyright Office.[6]

---

[5] U.S. Copyright Office Correspondence. (2023). Re: Zarya of the Dawn (Registration # VAu001480196). February 21, 2023. Available at https://www.copyright.gov/docs/zarya-of-the-dawn.pdf.

[6] Brittain, B. (2023). US Copyright Office denies protection for another AI-created image. *Reuters*. 6 September 2023. Available at: https://www.reuters.com/legal/litigation/us-copyright-office-denies-protection-another-ai-created-image-2023-09-06/.

The only key jurisdiction with copyright legislation that allows copyright protection of computer-generated works that do not have a human creator is the UK by its Copyright Designs and Patents Act 1988 ("CDPA"). Section 178 of the CDPA defines "computer-generated" to mean a work that "is generated by computer in circumstances such that there is no human author of the work." In such a circumstance, the protection is for 50 years from the end of the calendar year in which the work was made,[7] and under section 9(3), the author shall be taken to be the person who made the necessary arrangements to create the work. It could be argued that a user of a generative AI program could be regarded as the "person who made the necessary arrangements to create the work" through the use of the prompt to the AI system but it should be noted that this provision was first introduced in the 1980s and its meaning in the age of generative AI systems is not entirely clear.

In any case, s178 is not support for the proposition that under UK law that output generated by generative AI will automatically be protected by copyright law. There is a fundamental requirement, present in all jurisdictions, that needs to be present for copyright to subsist, that is, it must satisfy the threshold requirement of originality, which will be discussed in the following sections.

Despite the foregoing, copyright may be granted in cases where the creator can prove there was substantial human input in addition to what was produced by generative AI. This will also be discussed further in the following sections.

2.3. *Copyright law — Originality and Some Human Input*

This section will explore the concept of originality under the copyright law of a few key jurisdictions and apply the existing law and legal concepts to the technology of generative AI.

---

[7] Copyright Designs and Patents Act 1988 (UK) s12(7).

2.3.1. *Australia and Singapore*

The requirement of originality for copyright to subsist is present in most Western countries, due to one of the oldest treaties on copyright protection, the Berne Convention of 1886, which enshrined the originality element.

In Australia, the requirement of originality has never been a high threshold. All that is required is that it must have, firstly, originated from the author, and not copied from another work, and secondly, it has the requisite intellectual skill and effort put in to achieve the work.[8] The first requirement of originating from the author may be problematic given that the first step is the use of generative AI systems, thus clearly, it is not originating from the author.

In Singapore, the long-held test for originality was similar to that in Australia until the 2017 decision of *Global Yellow Pages Ltd v Promedia Directories Pte Ltd*[9] which stated the following[10]:

> For copyright to subsist in any literary work, there must be an authorial creation that is causally connected with the engagement of the human intellect ... A compiler must exercise sufficient creativity in selecting or arranging the material within the compilation; and if the compiler does so, the resulting copyright will only protect the original expression in the form of the selection or arrangement of the material.

Thus, in Singapore, the requirement for a literary work to be an "authorial creation that is causally connected with the engagement of the human intellect" appears to put the bar somewhat higher for the threshold for originality. Like Australia, it would appear that the creation must emanate from a person, and not from an AI system, and further, must show engagement of the human intellect. Thus, similar to the position in Australia, it would be difficult for output from an AI system to obtain copyright protection, even if there is subsequent human input.

---

[8] *IceTV Pty Limited v Nine Network Australia Pty Limited* [2009] HCA 14.
[9] *Global Yellow Pages Ltd v Promedia Directories Pte Ltd* [2017] SGCA 28.
[10] *Ibid.*, at [24].

2.3.2. *European Union and United Kingdom*

In the European Union ("EU"), the issue of the meaning of "original" needs to be examined in the context where a tool or device, such as a generative AI system, is used. In this regard, it is instructive to examine the concept of originality in light of the use of a tool such as a camera for photographic works.

The European Union Council Directive 93/98/EE of 1993 expressed that the meaning of the term "original" in the Berne Convention 1886 in relation to photographic work is satisfied "if it is the author's own intellectual creation reflecting his personality, no other criteria such as merit or purpose being taken into account."[11] Indeed, many jurisdictions have taken this approach of not evaluating any merit criteria of originality since the Berne Convention of 1886.

The Court of Justice of the European Union (CJEU) did however hold in the case of *Painer v Standard Verlags GmbH*[12] that originality is satisfied since the photographer "was able to express his creative abilities in the production of the work by making free and creative choices."[13] The CJEU went on to say that in portrait photography, the photographer can make free and creative choices in many ways and at various points in its production, such as choosing the background, the subject's pose, the lighting, the framing, the angle of view, and the atmosphere created.[14] All of these choices contribute to the photographer giving the final work his "personal touch."[15]

The CJEU concluded that in relation to a portrait photograph, the freedom available to the author to exercise his creative abilities will not necessarily be minor nor nonexistent.[16] As a result, the originality element is met and copyright protection is available.

---

[11] European Union Council Directive 93/98/EE of 1993, Recital 17 in the preamble.

[12] *Painer v Standard Verlags GmbH* (C-145/10) [2011] E.C.D.R. 13. 12 April 2011.

[13] *Ibid.*, at para 89.

[14] *Ibid.*, at para 90–92.

[15] *Ibid.*, at para 92.

[16] *Ibid.*, at para 93.

Applying the CJEU position to generative AI systems, what distinguishes a camera from a generative AI system is that a camera allows photographers to have plenty of room to vary its use, such as changing the lighting and the pose. A generative AI system, however, is a system that gives users limited choices, other than to express a prompt, such as "give me a picture of a fat man sitting on a wall next to a river." While the prompt can be more sophisticated than this and contain a lot more description, it still cannot measure up to the breadth of the free and creative choices available to a person using a camera.

Further, the requirement that it must be "the author's own intellectual creation reflecting his personality" before originality is satisfied may be difficult to achieve. Other than the prompt, what the generative AI system produces can hardly be "the author's own intellectual creation" as generative AI systems are more autonomous than they are mere tools like a camera with which one can express one's own intellectual creativity.

It remains to be seen if in future cases whether the CJEU will hold that if, after a work is created by a generative AI system, a person then stamps "his own personal touch" on the artwork by changing it, adding to it and so on, that might be sufficient expression of their free and creative choices to attract copyright protection.

In the UK, the originality test was previously similar to Australia's test, that of being able to show sufficient skill, labor, and judgment in the creation of the work. That was the case until CJEU case law brought in the separate test expounded above. However, post-Brexit, there is uncertainty over which test applies in the UK. From October 2021 to January 2022, the UK Intellectual Property Office held a public consultation on artificial intelligence and intellectual property. The UK government's decision after the public consultation to not make any changes to the legislation further fuels this uncertainty.

If UK courts revert to the sufficient skill, labor, and judgment test, while the output generated by generative AI systems by itself may not satisfy the skill, labor, and judgment test, if a person were to exercise his own skills, labor, and judgment on the output, such as changing it in a manner exhibiting the requisite skill, labor, and judgment, then there is a strong argument that copyright protection should be afforded.

It would have to be a case-by-case decision with much depending on the level of skill, labor, and judgment exercised. For example, if all that was done to the output was to change the color of the background, that would probably not meet the requirements of skill or judgment. However, if much more intricate and finessed changes were done that clearly demonstrated the exercise of great skill, then it would likely be open to a court to find originality and, hence, attract copyright protection.

2.3.3. *United States*

Despite the various decisions by the US Copyright Office to deny the registration of copyright for works generated solely by AI systems, significantly, in March 2023, the US Copyright Office issued a Guidance on works containing material generated by AI. The Guidance essentially restated the same position on output that is generated solely by AI systems but clarified that works created with the assistance of AI may be copyrightable if the work involves sufficient human authorship. The Guidance also specifically highlighted that "applicants have a duty to disclose the inclusion of AI-generated content in a work submitted for registration and to provide a brief explanation of the human author's contributions to the work."[17]

The Guidance gave some examples of when AI-generated material will have met the sufficient human authorship requirement to support a copyright claim. These include selecting or arranging AI-generated material in a sufficiently creative way that "the resulting work as a whole constitutes an original work of authorship,"[18]

---

[17] Copyright Registration Guidance: Works Containing Material Generated by Artificial Intelligence, 88 Fed. Reg. 16,190 (Mar. 16, 2023) (to be codified at 37 C.F.R. § 202).
[18] *Ibid.*, at 16,192.

modifying the output to such a degree that the modifications meet the standard for copyright protection.[19] However, the Guidance made clear that in these cases, copyright will only protect the human-authored aspects of the work, which are "independent of" and do "not affect" the copyright status of the AI-generated material itself. It is not entirely clear what is meant by this because, for the output of generative AI systems, most of the time, it may not be so easy to separate out the human-authored aspects of the work so that it is "independent of" the AI-generated material. For example, if the output of a generative AI system shows a little boy standing and a person modifies this to a little boy walking, can this be said to be "independent of" the AI-generated material itself? The Guidance appears to set a threshold requirement that is not terribly clear, nor achievable.

In another part of the Guidance, a more hopeful picture is presented where it states that one of the key considerations is whether the final work is a "mechanical reproduction" or the author's own original mental conception to which the author gave visible form.[20] If it is the latter, copyright will subsist. This gives hope that if outputs of generative AI systems have been sufficiently modified demonstrating the user's creative originality, then the Copyright Office will treat the generative AI system as more of a tool, like a camera, than an autonomous system.

3. Copyright Infringement by AI-Generated Output

One caveat that users of generative AI systems must be aware of when deploying its use is the possibility or propensity for the AI-generated output to infringe copyright. Generative AI systems are trained on massive amounts of data, including from data lakes, oftentimes without obtaining the appropriate licenses. A case in point is Stability AI, the creators of Stable Diffusion. Getty, an image licensing service, has commenced legal action against Stability AI

---

[19] *Ibid.*, at 16,193.

[20] *Ibid.*, at 16,192.

in both the UK and the US, alleging that it unlawfully copied and processed millions of images protected by copyright and the associated metadata owned or represented by Getty Images without a license.[21] At the time of writing in December 2023, The New York Times has commenced legal action against the owners of ChatGPT, OpenAI, and Microsoft for copyright infringement in using content belonging to The New York Times in the training of ChatGPT.

Depending on how the generative AI algorithm is programmed, it is possible that the system might produce output that is substantially similar to a copyrighted work and, hence, would constitute copyright infringement. There are two strategies that can be undertaken to minimize this from happening.

The first is to prompt the system to produce output based on works that are no longer protected by copyright, for example, "compose a ten-bar, thirty-second tune that sounds like Bach" or "create a picture with water lilies in the style of Monet for my flower business." This, however, is not foolproof as there may be modern-day artists who may have created such a water lilies picture that was used as training data for the AI system. Hence, the second strategy should, as a matter of best practice, always be employed, and this is simply to make alterations to the output so that there is human input that can render the final product to be not substantially similar to what the AI system churned out.

4. Conclusion

Generative AI systems can be used to assist organizations in their day-to-day operations, saving time and costs. In jurisdictions such as the UK and the US, there are substantive reasons to argue that the outputs of generative AI systems, when they have been modified by humans to a degree that demonstrates some skill or judgment, can attract copyright protection, thereby also increasing the intellectual assets of organizations. In jurisdictions such as Australia

---

[21] Getty Images Press Site — Newsroom — Getty Images. (2023). Getty Images Statement. Available at: https://newsroom.gettyimages.com/en/getty-images/getty-images-statement.

and Singapore, where copyright protection might not subsist for generative AI systems' outputs, generative AI systems can still be utilized to add value in the production of business and organizational assets, as well as to increase the productivity of processes and workflows through their time and cost savings.

Chapter 14

Concluding Thoughts

We started this book with a chapter on data strategy, as it should be the guiding vision and goal for all data-driven initiatives. In the opening chapter under the data strategy and governance theme, Legner and Pentek define data strategy and provide a checklist and recommendations on how to develop and implement a data strategy. The essential elements are elucidated. Importantly, a data strategy is not just a vision or mission statement that involves data. Such a statement would be insufficient and thus ineffective. A good data strategy needs to be both effective (in achieving desired outcomes) and *robust*. To be sustainable as a long-term plan, it must "foster synergies between diverse data-related activities" and align priorities and incentives among employees. Everyone has to see the same goal(s) and row in the same direction.

Next, Rosich and Rüst illustrate how data drive the changes in leadership methods and show that data are becoming an active tool, instead of a passive or reactionary tool, even in traditional businesses. Data "evolved from a mere commodity to a strategic force...." In order to shepherd and harness data as an active, strategic force, Rosich and Rüst (2024) recommend (a) what organizations must implement and (b) the attributes that organizations must nurture.

Data quality cannot be assumed. It has to be monitored and evaluated. The best strategy will be wasted if the organization has

211

poor-quality data to start with. It is important to realize that poor data quality is (often) not an IT problem; it is an organizational problem that needs to be managed at the whole-of -organization level. Ram Kumar explains a data quality framework that supports data quality best practices. Data governance can provide the oversight and management of data at an organizational level that institutes data quality and acceptable use of data.

The acceptable use of data can be viewed from the perspective of data governance and data privacy. Government regulations are often a response to data access and data privacy issues. Terry Ray discusses the modern demands on data security and consumer privacy. Often, the overemphasis on compliance, audits, and steep fines leads to siloed overprotection (that hinders even authorized users) and creates a false sense of security on (all) data. Instead, "an effective program to protect data" should be instituted, for which compliance with regulations for selected data would be a natural consequence. One should be aiming for security, not just compliance. Terry Ray proposes six basic questions and concludes that "organizations that can answer these questions rapidly, reliably, completely, and accurately have laid the groundwork for a very effective data security program."

With the increasing importance of data privacy, Sowmya explains data privacy problems and available solutions. A common concern is that privacy-enhanced data reduce the value and insights from those data. Sowmya explains the ways in which essential information from data can be shared even among different organizations (e.g., hospital, credit card company, and insurer) without revealing sensitive information. Ways to share data, computations, insights, and even AI models are explored. In AI models, federated learning can be used to share updated model coefficients from different companies without sharing the underlying data. The abstract AI model contains the insights but not the data, and all participating companies can use the AI model in their business (on localized company data) with far more superior performance than an AI model trained on only one company's data.

Learning from best practices on data adopted by other regions, Hartmann, Baumann, and Lederer open our eyes to the latest data-sharing initiatives spearheaded by the EU to link data-sharing necessities to ESG and sustainability. Dataspaces are introduced. The risks and opportunities associated with the commercial use of dataspaces are explained. Privacy concerns are cited as the principal barrier to data sharing among businesses.

Thereafter, we shift our attention to AI as a modern tool to extract insights from data and greatly increase the potential of data strategy.

The theme of AI value creation opens with a chapter on the rise of AI. Neumann Chew C.H. explains the variants of AI, where AI is successfully applied, and where it has spectacularly failed. Thereafter, Sachin Tonk explains the rise of generative AI. To help users understand the potential of GenAI, specific GenAI applications found in healthcare, finance, entertainment, and manufacturing are described. Sachin highlights the importance of answering two questions before embarking on GenAI projects. Do you need to generate content? What is the business value of the generated content?

Michael Taylor likens data to crude oil and AI to a refinery to explain the synergy between data and AI. He highlights the importance of optimizing the data-to-insight-to-action cycle for companies looking to leverage AI effectively and suggests four focus areas: (1) effective integration of data, (2) generating actionable tailored insights, (3) establishing a feedback loop to improve data and analysis, and (4) strengthening the loop to enable a quicker and more effective data-to-insight-to-action cycle. Mastering such a feedback loop is the key to long-term success.

A much more detailed AI value creation case study is provided of a digital bank. Chalee Asavathiratham presents a hybrid AI–human service model of an established bank. While AI is embedded in products and services, the human factor is intentionally designed into the service/product delivery and is irreplaceable by AI. "AI and humans are good at different things — blend their capabilities." One can redesign one's work processes by using AI to augment and support humans.

Finally, we conclude this book by examining the legal liability and risk arising from GenAI. AI-generated content is not the same as human-generated content. In particular, Prof. Lim notes that "copyright only protects the expression of ideas, not the ideas themselves," but GenAI is not an author. The amount and significance of human authorship are key factors in the consideration of copyright. While some companies try to claim copyright over GenAI-assisted content, at the same time, the GenAI output might infringe on copyright belonging to others. Several legal cases are presented to demonstrate that the opportunities of and risks to copyright are real. The recommended way to reduce the legal risk is for people to revise the GenAI output so that it is substantially different. But if too much human effort or time is required to revise GenAI output, then it might be faster and cheaper to not use GenAI in the first place. Thus, each business would need to assess the need, value, and risk of GenAI in specific applications and find the sweet spot that balances the speed of GenAI with the originality of humans.

The connection of ideas in this book can be summarized in the following flowchart:

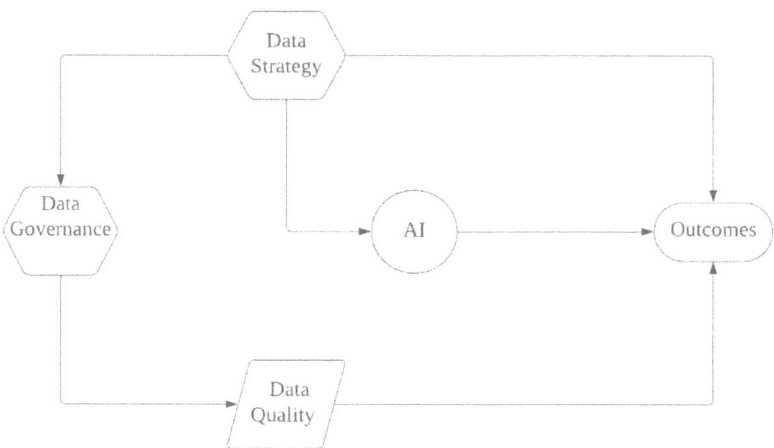

Data strategy provides the all-encompassing vision, goals, and support structure for all data-driven initiatives. The objective is to direct, support, and incentivize an organization's data efforts toward certain desirable business outcomes. For efforts and outcomes to be sustainable, data governance is necessary to manage the use and quality of data at the whole-of-organization level. The quality of data has a direct impact on outcomes. In these modern times, AI can be used as a strategic tool to greatly expand the potential outcomes of an ambitious data strategy. Potential outcomes may or may not be realized in spite of sophisticated data technologies and AI. The actual outcomes depend on humans orchestrating the processes, especially the clarity and commitment of the top management. Humans, not technology, are the critical factor in the success or failure of outcomes.

We hope you have enjoyed reading this book and have learned something new and useful. As we navigate a new era defined by rapid technological advancements, the integration of data strategy, governance, AI, and analytics becomes critically important for organizations. We hope the frameworks and best practices outlined in this book will prove useful to help your organization harness the transformative power of data and AI to make better decisions, improve your productivity, grow, and succeed.

About the Authors in Data Strategy and Governance

Christine Legner is a Professor of Information Systems at the Faculty of Business and Economics (HEC), University of Lausanne, Switzerland and an Academic Research Fellow at the MIT Center for Information Systems Research. Her research fields are data strategy and data management, enterprise architecture, and strategic IT planning. She is the co-Founder and Academic Director of the Competence Centers Corporate Data Quality (CC CDQ), an industry-funded research consortium and expert community. In the CC CDQ, she and the research team collaborate with industry experts from Fortune 500 companies to develop concepts, tools, and methods that advance data management. Together with Dr. Olivier Verscheure, she is co-Director of the Executive Certificate in Data Science and Management (CAS), a joint program offered by the University of Lausanne and the École Polytechnique Fédérale de Lausanne (EPFL). Professor Legner has published more than 150 peer-reviewed articles in academic journals and conference proceedings. She is the editor of the book *Strategic Enterprise Architecture Management* and she has co-authored eBooks on data strategy and data catalogs. She received a post-doctoral qualification (Habilitation) and a doctorate from the University of St.

Gallen (Switzerland) and has been a visiting researcher at INSEAD, Stanford University, and HEC Montreal.

Dr. Tobias Pentek is the Head of Community and Innovation in the Competence Center Corporate Data Quality (CC CDQ), an industry-funded research consortium and expert community in the field of data management. In the CC CDQ, he and the research team collaborate with industry experts from Fortune500 companies to develop concepts, tools and methods that advance data management. Tobias is also a data strategy consultant, a lecturer at the CDQ Data Management Academy, and a frequent speaker at data conferences. With his PhD from the University of St. Gallen, he is also the mind behind the CDQ Data Excellence Model, empowering organizations to structure and thrive in their data journeys. Tobias' contributions continue to drive data innovation, specifically in the field of data excellence for sustainability, data sharing approaches, and data quality.

Meri Rosich is a visionary leader driving impactful outcomes through data-driven strategies. With over 30 years of experience, she has spearheaded elite data teams across renowned organizations such as Bertelsmann, American Express, Samsung, NTT Docomo, Visa, and Standard Chartered. Originally from Barcelona, Meri has traveled the globe, living in dynamic cities like New York, London, and Hong Kong before settling in Singapore 15 years ago. Meri's academic journey reflects her commitment to continuous learning. She holds an MBA with special recognition from the London Business School and achieved a Ph.D. Summa cum Laude in Tech Strategy from the University of Barcelona, earning the prestigious Doctor Europeus honorific mention. She is also an Adjunct Professor of

Data Strategy and Sustainability at Globis University, a prestigious MBA program in Japan. Balancing corporate leadership with entrepreneurial ventures, Meri has founded four start-ups, leveraging both successes and setbacks as invaluable learning opportunities. Committed to fostering inclusive leadership and promoting data literacy, she actively mentors women to cultivate the next generation of technology trailblazers. She has contributed her expertise to various initiatives, including serving on the advisory board of the Data Literacy Project, mentoring fintech initiatives for the United Nations Development Programme, and advocating for women in STEM as ambassador for the UN Women STEM program. She co-founded the Female Founders think tank and the Women Data Leaders network, demonstrating her commitment to advancing gender equality in the tech industry. Meri's contributions have earned her widespread recognition, including being named among the "30 People Who Are Changing The World" by the London Business Review, as well as accolades such as Top 100 Chief Data Officer, 100 Women in Tech, Most Promising Female Developer, and the Moebius Digital Award.

Cat Rüst has over three decades of experience driving growth and innovation with a wealth of expertise in software development, business management, and strategic consultancy. Her proven track record of delivering exceptional results in highly competitive global markets demonstrates her strategic acumen and leadership capabilities. Throughout her career, Cat has championed transformative projects. As Global Head of Technology at Standard Chartered Bank, she innovated bank processes, expanded the tech portfolio by 22%, and established global tech partnerships while securing multibillion-dollar limits for hypergrowth companies. At UBS AG, Cat leveraged her experience in start-ups to build an ecosystem around the bank, resulting in innovative revenue streams across Greater China and the Asia-Pacific. As Founder, COO, and

Director of Exicon Ltd., Cat launched numerous successful technology ventures (from Saas to consulting and mobile apps) and managed multimillion-dollar product portfolios, underscoring her entrepreneurial spirit and vision. Her educational background includes a B.Sc. in Management and Statistics from the University of St. Andrews, complemented by certifications in business process engineering, marketing, and data science. Recognized as one of the top female entrepreneurs in fintech and a leader in the industry, Cat's passion for innovation and growth has earned her acclaim. Speaking multiple languages, including English, Mandarin, French, and German, Cat brings a global perspective to her endeavors, fostering collaboration and driving success. With her extensive experience, strategic acumen, and dedication to driving revenue and growth, Cat's most recent role as Chief Revenue Officer for Screening Eagle Technologies leveraged all of her previous skills to drive the business of "Protecting the built world" with cutting-edge technology.

Ram Kumar is the CDAO at CIGNA. He is a senior and seasoned strategic thought leader and executive with sound business acumen and skills in developing and executing business, data and analytics, AI, technology, and organizational transformation strategies of varying sizes and complexities. He had effectively and efficiently integrated people, data, processes, and technology coupled with the right organizational culture to create pragmatic and sustainable business outcomes. Ram has held senior executive roles such as CDAO, CDO, CIO, CTO, and CEO. He has successfully operated in different and dynamic market conditions in various industry verticals and government organizations in several regions including Australia, New Zealand, Europe, the Asia-Pacific, Latin America, the Middle East, Africa, and North America. In addition, he has successfully established businesses through international M&As

and JVs, and managed the IT and data functions. Ram has over 35 years of extensive IT experience (programming, commercial product development, strategy, architecture, and R&D to execution and operations management) and over 30+ years of "DATA" experience covering end-to-end data life cycle components including data strategy, data analytics, data quality, data governance, data monetization, meta and master data, data-driven culture, data privacy and ethics, and data risk management. Ram was an early adopter of AI since 1986 and is experienced in fundamental and applied AI research, development, and commercialization. He worked with AI pioneers, and built and deployed the first AI (explainable) commercial solution in 1986. His first big data (30-year data-set)-based AI/machine learning-driven advanced analytics solution was implemented for a large government agency in 1992. Ram has received several prestigious international/global awards for delivering fit-for-purpose business solutions that are innovative, best in class, and use the world's best practices to drive sustainable business outcomes.

Terry Ray is the Vice President of Product Strategy at Varonis. As VP, Terry uses his decades of data security expertise to support the data leader's innovation and development. He focuses on building technology that simplifies the decades-old complexities organizations face with legacy data security controls. Prior to joining Varonis, Terry worked at Imperva (acquired by Thales Inc.) for more than 22 years, holding positions such as Chief Technology Officer and SVP and Fellow. In these roles, Terry was responsible for developing and articulating the company's technical vision and strategy. He maintained a deep knowledge of application and data security solutions and the threat landscape. He also contributed to numerous data security projects to fulfill the security requirements of customers and regulators from every industry.

Terry is a frequent speaker for RSAC, FS-ISAC, Gartner, ISSA, OWASP, ISACA, IANS, CDM, NLIT, The American Petroleum Institute, and other professional security and audit organizations worldwide. Terry also provides expert commentary for the media and has been quoted in Security Week, SC Magazine, Forbes, CBS News, the BBC, and more.

Sowmya Ganapathi Krishnan is the Head of Data and AI Strategy and Governance, Thoughtworks APAC. In her current role, she works toward the vision of enabling businesses to become data-driven. She has more than 14 years of experience in the industry, which started with building low-latency trading systems, and architecting and building modern data platforms driving data strategy at scale. Her recent publication relates to data strategy for trusted public sector sharing in Singapore. Sowmya is a member of the SGTech Digital Trust Committee that focuses on establishing Singapore as a global node for digital trust. She leads the Privacy Enhancing Technology workgroup as part of the committee, focusing on building awareness, capability, and thought leadership in this space in Singapore and the region. Sowmya has a Master's degree in Software Engineering and has always remained a technologist at heart. She is passionate about leveraging data and tech for social good.

Marcus Hartmann is a Senior Executive Leader and Advisor. He has extensive experience in global business operations, specializing in digital and tech-enabled innovation combined with a strong acumen for commercial, performance, and functional impact. As a proven data and AI expert, he has spent his entire career in the digital data and analytics industry, helping companies to move more easily and quickly into a data-rich and tech-enabled world. He is building, scaling, and commercializing data, advanced analytics, and AI solutions. He is accomplished in spearheading large-scale digital transformation initiatives from inception to completion and well-versed in analyzing corporate performance, overseeing business modeling, and driving cost savings, revenue growth, and profitability improvements for high-worth clients. Adept at implementing and integrating cutting-edge digital technologies and platforms to streamline operations, enhance customer experiences, and drive business growth, he is also equipped with inclusive insights into growth-focused M&A, commercial due diligence, post-merger integration, and operational performance management.

He joined PwC in August 2019 and quickly established the function of Chief Data Office and a corresponding internal digital and delivery unit. He leads a team of data, software, and digital experts to establish and grow the foundations for efficient and scalable data use within the firm and the realization of highly scalable, market-oriented data products and new digital business models. Previously, he was Chief Data Officer for the entire Group at ProSiebenSat.1 Media SE and Chairman of the Executive Board of ProSiebenSat.1 Digital Data GmbH. In this role, he was responsible for all strategic and company-wide data and AI initiatives. He has also worked for Bisnode AB, one of the leading providers of digital business information, analytical services, and smart data analytics, based in Stockholm, for which he most recently served as Group Vice President. In this position, he was in charge of the group-wide functions of business intelligence, advanced analytics, and big data analytics. He also held various management positions at the global information services provider Experian, Arvato Infoscore, and Bertelsmann Financial Services. He is also a board member at the International Data Spaces Association (IDSA) and in the German digital association Bitkom e.V. in the working group "Data policy and data spaces."

Felix W. Baumann is an experienced Senior Manager in the Chief Data Office department of PwC Germany, directly supporting the CDO. Dr. Baumann has more than 10 years of post-qualification experience in science consultancy, digital transformation, and software development. He has been involved in numerous projects to strengthen and grow data and analytics capabilities by driving strategy, community-building, program management, and system development. He has authored multiple scientific articles exploring the interactive nature of both additive manufacturing processes and data and analytics. As a lecturer, he has taught and guided students at the University of Stuttgart and the Macromedia University of Applied Science.

Elisa Lederer is a Senior Associate at PwC Germany's Chief Data Office department. She has a background in European Studies and Economics and 5 years of postgraduate experience in stakeholder management, networking, and public affairs. At PwC, she is in charge of external outreach activities and thought leadership on data analytics topics. Elisa has contributed to different scientific publications and has worked as a lecturer at the Macromedia University of Applied Science in Düsseldorf, Germany.

About the Authors in AI Value Creation

Neumann Chew is a Senior Lecturer at Nanyang Business School, Nanyang Technological University, Singapore. He was previously the Principal and Head of Analytics at SAS Institute where he designed and led advanced analytics solutions for government agencies, banks, insurance companies, hospitals, and large corporations. Prior to that, he was Head of Research and Statistics at the Ministry of Health and Professor of Financial Mathematics at Dubai Academic City. He teaches Analytics and Machine Learning to undergraduates and postgraduates who specialize in analytics, as well as corporate executives. He wrote the textbook *Artificial Intelligence, Analytics and Data Science* published by Cengage and used in universities globally, including a Chinese translation for the China market.

Sachin Tonk is currently the Deputy Chief Data Officer at GovTech and leads talented data and analytics teams. GovTech empowers Singapore through infocomm technology and related engineering technology, playing a vital role in materializing Singapore's vision of becoming a Smart Nation. For the past 19 years, Sachin has established global data and analytics teams for global organizations to enable business growth and achieve organizational KPIs. He has a diverse professional exposure in international settings across India, Singapore, the United Kingdom, and the Middle East. He has an outstanding track record in automation, artificial intelligence, data analytics, business intelligence, innovation, business transformation, governance, and architecture. Sachin holds an MBA degree from the National University of Singapore and the Anderson School of Management. He has successfully launched his podcast "Making Data Speak" where the latest data- and AI-related topics are discussed by industry leaders. He has won several data and analytics awards including the "Indian Achievers Award." He is also a Senior Adjunct Lecturer at NUS, teaching the module "Transforming Organizations with Data Storytelling."

Michael Taylor is the Technology, Data, and AI Officer at Siemens Mobility Digital Services. His primary responsibility is to shape the technology, data, and AI strategies. He plays a pivotal role in driving innovation, developing and implementing scalable rail IOT products and solutions, and leveraging data and AI technologies to enhance operational efficiency to deliver value for Siemens's rail customers. Prior to that, he was the AI Chief Data Scientist at the Siemens Mobility Rail Analytics Center in Singapore, with a mission to democratize data science and AI, and design innovative solutions to solve customers' business problems. Michael is a Fellow of the Royal Statistical Society and a Member of the Operations Research Society, and has been a Guest Lecturer of Big Data for Business Analytics at Bocconi University in Milan since 2019.

Chalee Asavathiratham is the Chief Digital Banking Officer at Siam Commercial Bank, Thailand, where he is in charge of the bank's digital transformation and digital revenue. Prior to joining SCB, he was the Chief Research Officer at WorldQuant, in charge of research teams and data scientists in 14 countries worldwide. He also served as a Quantitative Trader and Portfolio Manager at Merrill Lynch, New York, and Sun Trading, Chicago. He was a Management Consultant at McKinsey & Company in Bangkok and London and an Analytics Engineer at Pivotal Systems Corporation. Dr. Asavathiratham was awarded the King's Scholarship for his undergraduate, graduate, and doctorate degrees, all in Electrical Engineering and Computer Science from the Massachusetts Institute of Technology (MIT).

Associate Professor **Hannah Yee-Fen LIM** is an Associate Professor of Business Law at NTU. She is uniquely qualified with double degrees in Law and Computer Science from the University of Sydney. She is an internationally recognized legal expert in all areas of technology law, including IP, data protection, AI, Blockchain, FinTech, Cryptoassets, NFTs, health technology, cybersecurity and ethics. She is an appointed Legal Expert by international bodies, including the WHO and UNCITRAL advising on areas including AI and FinTech. Hannah is one of 15 international legal experts appointed by UNIDROIT on its Digital Assets Project Working Group. She also serves, by invitation, as a Legal Expert on the Law Commission of England and Wales Expert Advisory Panel on its Digital Assets Project concerning Cryptoassets and NFTs. She is the author of six scholarly books published by publishers such as Oxford University Press, including pioneering books on *Cyberspace Law* (2002) and *Autonomous Vehicles and the Law* (2018). She has authored hundreds of papers and her research has been cited with approval by the High Court of Australia and the Singapore Court of Appeal. She is currently PI or co-PI in grants on data and AI totaling more than S$57 million.

About the Editors

Wai Fong Boh is President's Chair and Professor of Information Systems at Nanyang Technological University (NTU), Nanyang Business School (NBS), Singapore. She is currently the Vice President for Lifelong Learning and Alumni Engagement at NTU. She is also the Director of the Information Management Research Centre at NBS, and she serves as co-Director for the NTU Centre in Computational Technologies for Finance (CCTF). She received her Ph.D. from the Tepper School of Business at Carnegie Mellon University. Her research interests are in the areas of innovation and technology management. She has published in leading journals, including Management Science, MIS Quarterly, and Academy of Management Journal. She is currently the Senior Editor of MIS Quarterly and has previously been the Associate Editor of Management Science and ISR. Furthermore, she is currently on, or has been on, the editorial board of multiple leading information systems journals. She was recently awarded Singapore's Public Administration Medal (Silver) and published a book *Identifying Business Opportunities through Innovation*. In 2023, she received the AIS Fellow Award and the AIS Sandra Slaughter Service Award.

Neumann Chew is a Senior Lecturer at Nanyang Business School, Nanyang Technological University, Singapore. He was previously the Principal and Head of Analytics at SAS Institute where he designed and led advanced analytics solutions for government agencies, banks, insurance companies, hospitals, and large corporations. Prior to that, he was Head of Research and Statistics at the Ministry of Health and Professor of Financial Mathematics at Dubai Academic City. He teaches Analytics and Machine Learning to undergraduates and postgraduates who specialize in analytics, as well as corporate executives. He wrote the textbook *Artificial Intelligence, Analytics and Data Science* published by Cengage and used in universities globally, including a Chinese translation for the China market.

Thara Ravindran is currently a Research Fellow at the Information and Management Research Center (IMARC), Nanyang Business School, NTU. Dr. Ravindran has a Ph.D. in Information Systems from NTU and an M.Sc. in Knowledge Management (Lexis-Nexis Gold Medal winner). Over the years, Dr. Ravindran has worked on several projects in the areas of entrepreneurship, innovation, and strategy. This includes an NRF-funded project that examined the effects of innovation practices of SMEs and start-ups on firm performance and the development of a global robotics strategy for a leading multinational. Dr. Ravindran's most recent research examined the usability and adoption of delivery robots which unearthed key insights into the adoption of such robots in the context of food delivery. Dr. Ravindran has also co-authored a recent book titled *Business Opportunity Identification Through Innovation*, which serves as a handbook for entrepreneurs, besides papers on topics related to innovation in entrepreneurship and robotic usability.

Index